Railway Memories

SELBY & GOOLE

This book is dedicated to the memory of Ernie Sanderson

BELLCODE BOOKS
10 RIDGE BANK
TODMORDEN
WEST YORKSHIRE OL14 7BA

Edited by Stephen Chapman

Printed by the Amadeus Press Ltd., Cleckheaton, West Yorks.

ABOVE: Standing like an ancient monument, the coaling tower at Goole motive power depot on 28th January, 1968, six months after the end of steam there. *Adrian Booth*

FRONTISPIECE: One of the handsome ex-North Eastern B16/1 class 4-6-0s, No. 61456, trundles a class H goods off Selby swing bridge and towards the station on 9th June, 1960. *Robert Anderson*

For their valued assistance *with the production of this book, our thanks are due to Robert Anderson, Ron Hollier, David Holmes, The Industrial Railway Society, The North Eastern Railway Association, The staff of Goole Museum, Goole Reference Library and Selby Reference Library, the late Sydney Martin, Tony Ross and all those who contributed photographs.*

INTRODUCTION

Railway Memories No.14 concentrates on Selby, Goole and surrounding areas like the important lines south from York to Church Fenton and Burton Salmon, plus the Isle of Axholme Railway, that lightly used system which meandered around the fertile but windswept flood plains east of Goole.

Selby may not be York or Doncaster, but it was once an important junction on the East Coast main line; a wonderful place to watch those trains which connected Britain's east and west coasts as they crossed the famous expresses connecting the North and South.

Goole, with its maize of lines winding around the docks, was quite different. Off the beaten track yes, but the variety of the shunt and trip engines used there is the stuff of legend.

The Axholme Joint was one of those self-contained railways with a character all of its own. Had history taken a different course in the late 1960s, it would now be carrying 1,000-ton coal trains to a huge power station.

Another highly individual railway crossing the area was the Hull & Barnsley, but Railway

Memories No.12 was devoted to it so little more will be said about it in this book.

Finally, as this book was being prepared for publication, the railway photographer Ernest Sanderson sadly died at the age of 89. As the author of Railway Memories No.1 back in 1988, Ernie pioneered the series.

Railway Memories No.14 covers a part of the country where Ernie loved to take photographs, often during his 'snap' break while at work with his permanent way gang, so it is fitting that it should be dedicated to his memory. He will be missed by many, forgotten by few.

Over the years, an amazing variety of shunters and trip locos has been allocated to Goole but the ex-Lancashire & Yorkshire "Pug" 0-4-0STs were the stalwarts of the dock lines in the steam age. No.51222 shunts the docks near Bridge Street level crossing in the 1950s. The imposing building on the left is the former L&Y goods offices completed in 1892. *N.E.Stead collection*

SETTING THE SCENE

The relatively level expanse of countryside that stretches from the urban heart of West Yorkshire to the River Humber provides the railways with few natural obstacles. Not in this part of the world are there the 1 in 60-odd gradients, circuitous curves and long tunnels of the Pennine region just the other side of Leeds.

Apart from the formidable barrier presented by the tidal and navigable River Ouse, there was little else to get in the railway builders' way and so the railways were able to follow the straightest and levellest of courses. Indeed, part of the Selby-Hull line is the longest stretch of dead straight railway in Britain.

Most of the railways hereabouts were built with two main purposes in mind - to link increasingly industrial West Yorkshire with the Humber ports, and to provide fast, direct routes between the North and London. As a result, the main lines developed into a North-South/East-West grid pattern.

Selby, the first crossing point of the great River Ouse for both road and rail, is dominated by its abbey, famous as one of the few to escape Henry V111's purges. A major junction on the East Coast main line until 1983, this market town combined maritime and agricultural industries, building North Sea trawlers while producing flour, cattle feeds and sugar.

Goole was nothing more than a tiny hamlet until the 1820s when the town and its docks were built from scratch by the Aire & Calder Navigation company. It was the success of this enterprise which caused the railways to happen.

With its Knottingley & Goole Canal the Navigation was able to carry goods directly by boat from the burgeoning West Yorkshire factories to ships in its own port at Goole. It now seemed an awful lot further and a lot more trouble to take goods to and from Hull, especially when it had to be done by horse and cart. Not suprisingly there was considerable consternation among the city's business community over the prospect of Goole creaming off their shipping trade. What Hull needed was a much faster link with West Yorkshire, and the railway - the transport of the future - seemed to be the answer.

The Leeds & Hull Railroad had already been formed in 1824 as part of a proposal to build a line all the way from Liverpool to Hull but it

failed to win enough support and was shelved. It was not until September, 1834 that Yorkshire's first main line was actually completed, and then it did not go to Hull. The Leeds and Selby Railway's promoters believed the rivers Ouse and Humber provided a cheaper alternative between Selby and Hull so the line ran just 20 miles from its Marsh Lane terminus in Leeds to Selby. There, on the south bank of the Ouse, it terminated at a station and jetty where passengers and goods for Hull and York were transferred to packet boats.

The next railway on the scene ran north to south, passing under the Leeds & Selby on its way. By July, 1840, the York and North Midland, led by the ruthless Railway King, George Hudson, had completed its line from York to Normanton where it joined the North Midland Railway which had been built at the same time from Leeds to Derby. These railways were vital links in a chain designed to give Hudson a main line from York to London Euston. The YNM passed through Church Fenton, Sherburn-in-Elmet, Milford, Burton Salmon and Castleford. It included a curve from Sherburn up to the Leeds & Selby at York Junction(Gascoigne Wood) - allowing through running between York and Selby - a curve from York Junction to Milford - enabling trains to run direct between Selby and the Castleford direction which ultimately allowed through running to the North Midland's Leeds terminus at Hunslet Lane.

A complete Leeds-Hull railway was achieved on the same day as the York & North Midland when the Hull & Selby Railway via Staddlethorpe and Howden was formally opened. At Selby, it needed an iron Bascule lifting bridge to cross the Ouse and a new through station. The original Leeds & Selby terminus became a goods depot, a role it kept until the 1980s. Together, the Leeds & Selby and the Hull & Selby formed the first complete east-west route through the region.

In 1847, the YNMR created the junction at Church Fenton when it opened a banch to Tadcaster and Wetherby. The following year it created Barlby North Junction, just outside Selby on the Hull line, by opening the line to Market Weighton, a small market town nestling at the foot of the Yorkshire Wolds. By now the

This was the end of the line so far as the Leeds & Selby Railway was concerned. Its original terminus of 1834 still stands on the south bank of the River Ouse 162 years after it was replaced by the present station.

The old station had six tracks, the outer pairs for goods extended out through the large doors and over the road onto a jetty where they were connected via wagon turntables by lines running parallel to the quayside. The centre pair, for passengers, terminated inside the building. Two other sidings east of the building served a coal depot and also extended onto a jetty.

Railway Mania was in full swing and a rail network was beginning to emerge.

A second east-west route was in the making with the intention of forging a direct rail link between West Yorkshire and Goole. This was the Wakefield, Pontefract & Goole Railway whose name amply describes the route, much of which shadowed the afore-mentioned canal to terminate by Goole docks in Aire Street. The WPG connected at Wakefield with the Manchester & Leeds Railway, making a line all the way from Goole to Liverpool and by the time the Goole line opened in April, 1848, the two companies had merged to become the Lancashire & Yorkshire Railway.

Two months later, the L&Y completed the branch south from Knottingley to Askern, just north of Doncaster. There it met head-on with the Great Northern Railway which was pushing relentlessly northwards from London. Besides giving the L&Y access to Doncaster, running powers gave the GNR direct access to West Yorkshire and brought it within 18 miles of York.

The GN reached York in 1852 when the YNMR obliged by opening its three-mile Burton Salmon-Knottingley branch and so completing a through route from Doncaster via Askern, Knottingley, Burton Salmon and Church Fenton - the first East Coast main line.

Economic recession then gripped the country, the railway building bubble burst and the next line was not opened until the 1860s, by which time the extreme rivalries of the Railway Mania had given way to a new spirit of co-operation.

The YNMR had merged with other companies in 1854 to form the North Eastern Railway which agreed to build a line south from Staddlethorpe to Goole and Thorne after several other company's attempts had foundered. The Manchester, Sheffield & Lincolnshire Railway(to become the Great Central) agreed to build a connection from Thorne North station to its own Doncaster-Grimsby line at Thorne Juntion. Completed in 1869, the new line created a direct route between Hull and Doncaster, replacing a long detour via Selby and Milford. For 10 years Goole had two stations until the L&Y transferred its services from Aire Street to the NER station in Boothferry Road.

This line features the region's most spectacular civil engineering structure of all, the 830ft-long Goole swing bridge over the swirling waters of the River Ouse, much wider and more treacherous here than at Selby.

A relatively short but highly significant line opened by the NER in 1869 was the five miles from Church Fenton to the Leeds & Selby at Micklefield. Rising up from the Vale of York at 1 in 133-145, it formed one of the area's more taxing gradients. It was part of a major project by

At the southern end of the NER's Staddlethorpe-Thorne line is Thorne North station, seen here looking towards Goole in 1961. At this time, the station signs were in the tangerine colour of BR's North Eastern Region but south of here they were in the dark blue of the Eastern Region. The goods yard, closed in 1965, was occupied by a steel fabrication and boat building works in 2001 while the signal box is no more, though the passenger station remains open. *Peter Cookson*

the NER and the London & North Western Railway which transformed the local railway scene into that which we recognise today. It included the line from the old Leeds & Selby terminus at Marsh Lane to a grand new through station in Leeds, called Leeds New station (later Leeds City.) Through trains could now run between Liverpool, Manchester, Leeds and Hull or York, and the die was cast for the Trans-Pennine expresses that would be such a key element of the area's principal passenger services.

Two years later, co-operation between the NER and the GNR - set to become firm partners in operating the East Coast route - saw the NER open the direct route between Doncaster, Selby and York. From January, 1871 Selby was on the East Coast main line linking London with Scotland and the GN no longer had to send its trains via Knottingley.

The new line left the GN's Doncaster-Askern branch at Shaftholme Junction, immediately north of which was Joan Croft. Here, a short east-facing spur was added in 1877 which provided direct running between the North and Goole and Grimsby, a line which was to prove its worth in modern times following the expansion

of steel making in Scunthorpe and the oil refineries and docks at Immingham. A connection was also laid from the Selby-Doncaster section to the Wakefield-Goole line which passed underneath but it seems to have been little used and abandoned at an early stage, though the earthworks are still clearly visible from ECML and Leeds-Goole trains in 2002.

In 1885 the Hull & Barnsley Railway opened. It crossed the River Ouse on a swing bridge at Drax, between Selby and Goole, and laid a connecting curve to the L&Y Knottingley-Goole line at Hensall Junction before passsing over the Selby-Doncaster line near Heck. Crossing over the Wakefield-Goole line just west of Snaith was the H&B and Great Central Joint line which, opened in 1916, ran to Doncaster from the H&B main line at Gowdall.

As the 19th century passed into the 20th, several minor lines were opened, such as the 4.5 mile Cawood, Wistow & Selby Light Railway in 1898 serving farming communities. It had its own Selby station at Brayton Gates until 1904 when trains were redirected to the main station following the line's takeover by the NER.

A more extensive set of minor lines was the

Goole & Marshland Railway opened between 1900 and 1904 to tap coal reserves in the flat countryside east of Goole. By the time it opened it had become the Isle of Axholme Railway run jointly by the NER and L&Y. It left the Goole-Doncaster line at Marshland Junction and ran to Reedness Junction where it divided, lines then running south to the Doncaster-Lincoln line at Haxey, and east to a terminus at Fockerby, just west of the River Trent. A branch to Hatfield Moor was opened in 1909 to serve a peat works which was still in production in 2002. The coal traffic never materialised and the line spent its entire life serving local farms.

But coal traffic was growing elsewhere and the NER had to expand its facilities for moving ever increasing tonnages to Hull for shipping. It opened a new marshalling yard at Gascoigne Wood in 1907 where coal from South and West Yorkshire pits was collected for forwarding to the port. Five years later, it opened a 10.5-mile single track from Thorpe Willoughby, east of Gascoigne Wood, to Goole in anticipation of coal traffic to the docks there. Passing over the ECML and the H&B, it included a connection from the Selby-Doncaster line at Brayton Junction while at the Goole end it joined the Oakhill Junction-Boothferry Road line, opened by the NER in 1910 to avoid the congested L&Y approaches to Goole.

In 1913, the wholly independent Derwent Valley Light Railway was opened throughout from York Layerthorpe to Cliffe Common station, just 3.25 miles outside Selby on the Market Weighton branch. A few years later, a one-mile line was laid from Howden station to airship sheds where the R100 was built in the 1920s.

These might have been the last acts but the combination of coal and electricity were to see more railways built in modern times. New lines built in the 1960s to serve the big three new power stations at Ferrybridge, Eggborough and Drax included reopening of the closed Hull & Barnsley from Hensall Junction to Drax power station in 1970.

Following the oil crisis of the early 1970s, the National Coal Board decided to mine huge reserves found in an eight to 11ft thick seam of good quality Barnsley coal deep beneath the arable farmlands west and north of Selby. But around four million tons lay smack underneath the Selby-York section of the East Coast main line. Mining was planned start in the 1980s but it would cause damaging subsidence to the railway resulting in severe speed restrictions that would wreck British Rail's high speed timetables. The NCB, on the other hand, would lose many millions of pounds in revenue and extra costs if a mile wide pillar of coal was left to support the railway. In fact, that coal was so precious to the NCB that it was prepared to pay for a new high speed main line around it - the third version East

One of Goole's Ivatt Class 2 2-6-0s rests at Fockerby while working a brakevan tour of the Axholme Joint. The old passenger platform is on the right. *Hugh Davies*

Coast main line to date. The British Railways(Selby Diversion) Bill was presented to Parliament in 1977 and received the Royal Assent on 26th July, 1979.

Laid out for 125mph running, the Selby Diversion stretches 14 miles from Colton, on the York-Normanton/Leeds line where the country's first 125mph double line junction was installed, to Temple Hirst, five miles south of Selby on the Doncaster line. It passes under the Leeds & Selby at Hambleton where a new junction has been created with north-east and south-west curves. Civil engineering features include a 26-span concrete viaduct carrying the new line over the River Wharfe at Ryther, an eight-span viaduct over Selby Dam, major bridges over the River Aire and Selby Canal, and realignment of the Leeds & Selby at Hambleton onto a new embankment with 1 in 140 gradients to lift it over the new line.

The Colton-Hambleton East section opened in May, 1983 when York-Selby-Hull trains became the first passenger services to use it, and the remainder at 60mph on 3rd October. The Selby-York line closed on 24th September, ECML trains being diverted via Knottingley in the meantime. Full 125mph running over the diversion began in May, 1984.

Although the line was built to avoid mining subsidence, it also had the advantage to BR of avoiding Selby swing bridge with its speed restrictions and tendancy to jam open to river traffic - in the 1950s it was being opened six to eight times a day and could be open for 20 to 30 minutes.

During the late 1980s, the Selby Diversion was electrified as part of the East Coast electrification. The overhead wires were energised on 17th September, 1989, the first King's Cross-York electric train to carry passengers running on 23rd September hauled by new Class 91 loco No. 91003.

At the same time as the diversion was being built, steps were taken to cater for an expected 10 million tons a year output which would be brought to the surface at Gascoigne Wood via underground links from the coalfield's Wistow, Riccall, Stillingfleet, North Selby and Whitemoor mines. A central railhead was established on the site of Gascoigne Wood yard where three rapid loading bunkers capable of loading up to 50 1,000-ton trains every 24 hours would dominate the scene. At Milford, the Gascoigne Wood curve was slewed outwards to accommodate six single-ended and six double-ended sidings intended to take over Gascoigne Wood's role of stabling empty coal wagons. Signalling was modernised and the line from just short of Church Fenton to Fryston, near Castleford, brought under the control of Milford signal box.

Worthy of mention is the ill-fated Thorne Colliery where a 9ft thick Barnsley seam was discovered more than half a mile underground in 1908. The pit was expected to produce a million and a half tons of coal a year. Sinking began in 1909 but because of the first world war and

One of the first trains to use the Colton-Hambleton section of the new Selby Diversion, a Cravens 2-car Class 105 DMU forming a road learning special for drivers in May, 1983. It has just left Hambleton North Junction and is returning to York. This was one of a series of photos BR handed out to the press at the time to illustrate progress on the project.

flooding the first coal was not wound until 1925. The colliery was to have been connected by its own five-mile railway to a proposed new wharf east of Goole at Swinefleet, but the plans were strongly opposed and all production left by a connection to the Thorne-Goole line instead. For a time it was one of the most productive pits in Yorkshire, winding a million tons a year but in 1956 the water problems returned and it closed for shaft relining. Twenty years later the Coal Board announced that it would reopen the mine with entirely new shafts. The new superstructure still stood in 2001 but with the run-down of British coal mining there seems little chance that Thorne will wind coal again. The single line rail connection from the main line was removed in the early 1970s.

Narrow gauge railways were used by the Yorkshire Water Authority until 1982 for maintaining flood defences along the River Ouse between York, Selby and Goole. A major scheme in 1972-75 was at Asselby, near Howden, which required a 1.5-mile line and five locomotives to deliver materials for flood embankments. It included five passing loops and used good quality track allowing 20mph running. Until 2000, extensive 3ft gauge railways carried peat from Thorne Moors, as they still do in 2002 at Hatfield Moors a little further south. A tileworks at Escrick used a short narrow gauge line to carry clay from the claypits until 1979, as did another at Hemingbrough until closing in 1985.

Over the years, the railways have undergone several changes in administration and ownership. In 1923, the many different railway companies were grouped into just four big undertakings. The L&Y went to the London Midland & Scottish Railway while the North Eastern, Great Northern and Great Central joined the London & North Eastern Railway. These companies were nationalized on 1st January, 1948 and the railways brought under the control of British Railways which was divided into regions roughly following the lines of the old companies. Former LNER lines came under the North Eastern Region, and ex-LMS lines such as Wakefield-Goole under the London Midland Region for operating purposes until 1957 when they were transferred to the NE Region. Everything south of Shaftholme Junction was in the Eastern Region. In 1965 British Railways shortened its name to British Rail, and in 1967

the North Eastern and Eastern regions were merged to form a new Eastern Region managed from the NE headquarters in York.

During the 1990s the railways were de-nationalized and are now run by a complicated host of private companies. Most East Coast main line expresses are run by the Great North Eastern Railway which has endeavoured to incorporate some of the old LNER panache into its modern electric high speed trains. All local services are operated by Arriva Trains Northern. The main freight operators are Freightliner, and English Welsh & Scottish Railway which also operates postal trains and provides locomotives and crews for special workings. Track, signalling, structures and control of operations are the responsibility of Railtrack but in October, 2001 the company was put under the control of government-appointed administrators and just who or what will be responsible for the future stewardship of the railways' infrastructure is unclear.

Passenger services

With the East Coast main line passing through this part of Yorkshire - by three different routes in its time - it is fair to say that some of the world's most famous trains have sped across the landscape hereabouts - and still do. Names like The Flying Scotsman, The Aberdonian, and The Elizabethan conjure up images of streamlined A4 Pacifics rumbling over the swing bridge at Selby and charging south along the plain to Doncaster on their way between the Scottish and English capitals.

From the immediate post-war years right up to the 1980s, the number of weekday expresses each way on the ECML between York and Doncaster remained at round 20-plus, with extras on such busier days as Fridays. In the summer 1955 working timetable the Flying Scotsman was shown to pass through Selby at 1pm northbound and 1.59pm southbound(2.5 southbound on Saturdays.) Adding to the lunchtime spectacle was the one train which probably topped the 'Scotsman" in the excitement stakes, The Elizabethan, booked through Selby in summer 1955 at 12.18pm northbound(12.30 on Saturdays) and 1.22pm southbound(1.44 on Saturdays.) On Mondays to Fridays this train ran non-stop between King's Cross and Edinburgh and guarenteed a corridor tender A4 Pacific so that it could change footplate crews without stopping. Passing through southbound at various late morning times depending on which day it was, and at 12.5pm northbound, was The Norseman which ran between King's Cross and Newcastle's Tyne Commission Quay where it connected with sailings to Scandinavia. Just after half-past two on Fridays and Saturdays was the northbound Scarborough Flyer. Completing the procession of 1950s named expresses were The Northumbrian, The Heart of Midlothian, The Fair Maid, The Tees-Tyne Pullman, The Talisman, The Continental - a 1950s car-carrying sleeper service which ran from Newcastle to Dover on Wednesday nights and returned on Friday nights - and the daytime Anglo-Scottish Car Carrier with its name amblazoned on the sides of its enclosed car-carrying vans.

Coming up from the Eastern counties via Doncaster were the Colchester-York, Lowestoft-York and Colchester-Glasgow trains with similar southbound workings. Other expresses included the 6.30pm York-Swindon which, departing Selby at 6.52pm in summer, 1957, ran via Doncaster and Sheffield Victoria.

The 1950s were the decade of National Service and some expresses were virtually troop trains taking thousands of young servicemen around the country to or from leave or between postings. One specific troop train in summer 1955 was the unadvertised 3.45pm Fridays Only Catterick Camp-King's Cross, booked to pass Selby at 5.34pm.

From 1958, English Electric Type 4 diesels were introduced to East Coast main line services but steam was to enjoy its so-called "Indian Summer" when Gresley Pacifics modified with double chimneys and other improvements outperformed the rather overweight and feeble Type 4s. Then, in 1962 a new era began when the 3,300hp Deltic diesels entered service and they were up to the job, just 22 replacing 55 Pacifics and within a couple of years steam was all but eliminated from the ECML. The 1960s saw 100mph running, new coaching stock, tumbling journey times, the Inter-City brand and increasing patronage.

The Beeching era of the 1960s saw many changes and cuts but in summer, 1968 the overnight train between Colchester and Glasgow still ran, as did the daytime Colchester-Newcastle while a Yarmouth-York had replaced the Lowestoft train. A long-standing Sheffield Victoria-York train had become Sheffield Midland-York with the general rundown of Sheffield Victoria station. But the Elizabethan

There was no finer sight in steam days than a famous East Coast express hauled by a named Pacific loco. Here, A1 No. 60155 *Borderer* pounds through Selby station in August, 1961 with the King's Cross-Newcastle 'Northumbrian,' unfortunately minus headboard or any other identification, as was often the case by the 1960s. *Peter Cookson / N. E. Stead collection.*

The 11.42pm York-Doncaster seemed to be regularly double-headed. On a dull 24th May, 1961, B1 4-6-0 No. 61138 of Sheffield Darnall shed was piloting Doncaster-based sister No. 61001 *Eland* as the train passed Brayton, just south of Selby. *Peter Rose.*

was no more, having made its last non-stop run on 9th September, 1962 because there was no way the Deltics could change crews on the move.

The late 1970s saw the ECML enter another phase as the InterCity 125 High Speed Trains began to replace the Deltics. As a new 125 timetable was introduced on 8th May, 1978, train speeds were raised to 125mph and journey times slashed. Even so, the timetable still remained at around 20 or so daytime expresses in each direction and of those, five northbound and four southbound were York-King's Cross semi-fasts, to which the Deltics were relegated but which probably gave Selby its best ever direct service to and from London. All that remained of the Eastern Counties trains by now, however, was a summer Saturday Newcastle-Yarmouth each way. Selby's new-found London service was not to last. When the Selby Diversion opened in 1983, the York-Selby line closed and all ECML services avoided the town. It was not until 2000 that Selby regained a regular London service. First when Great North Eastern Railway rerouted its daily Hull-Kings Cross train via Selby in May, and then in September when new company Hull Trains introduced its own Hull-Selby-Kings Cross service of three trains each way every weekday and one on Sundays.

In 2001, the new ECML carried twice as many expresses though these include Cross-Country services switched from the York-Sheffield lines in the 1980s.

Until the 1980s around eight overnight and sleeping car trains passed through Selby in each direction - trains like The Aberdonian, The Night Scotsman and The Tynesider. A new named overnight train, a cut-price seated King's Cross-Aberdeen/Glasgow service called The Nightrider was introduced in May, 1982 and proved successful but overnight trains were already being withdrawn or switched to the West Coast.

For the East Coast expresses, Selby was just a minor nuisance, hardly any of them calling there during the week except when brought to an unscheduled halt by the swing bridge. A good few more trains called there on summer Saturdays though. Perhaps the most important weekday train to call during the mid-1950s was the 7.53am Sunderland-King's Cross which departed at 10.7am, a train limited to 400 tons maximum. The Eastern Counties trains were more loyal servants, including the Down overnight Colchester-Glasgow which called around midnight. Otherwise, Selby had to mostly rely on a handful of York-Doncaster expresses and a few York-Doncaster and York-Selby stopping trains which also served the small intermediate stations. They included a daily train from Rowntrees chocolate factory in York which ran until the 1980s. A halt was provided at Joan Croft Junction for local railway staff and their families and on Saturdays in summer, 1955 the 6.27am Darlington-Doncaster called there to pick up(and set down when required), and the 11.2am Doncaster-York to set down. In May, 1984, the York-Doncaster local service was improved to 11 trains each way following the loss of the London trains, the new service travelling via Hambleton Junction and reversing at Selby. Over the following years, however, the Selby-Doncaster local service was whittled down to just the odd train each way.

Ever since the London & North Western Railway first ran Liverpool-Hull expresses in 1893, the Hull-Selby-Leeds line has been a key part of the trans-Pennine route. Also, the line has traditionally provided Selby with the bulk of its passenger services. In summer, 1950 it carried 22 westbound and 23 eastbound trains on Mondays to Fridays, including three Hull to Liverpool expresses and two from Liverpool to Hull. Semi-fast and stopping trains ran between Hull and Leeds along with stopping trains between Hull and Selby and Selby and Leeds. There was also a Hull-Bradford Forster Square express each way, and a Bridlington-Leeds train each way via the Market Weighton line, while the 5.7pm Leeds-Hull detached through carriages for Bridlington at Selby. Other interesting services included the 2.55pm Hull-Leeds stopping train which had the luxury of a buffet car on Saturdays, and the 8.35pm Hull to Leeds express which detached a portion at Selby for Pontefract Baghill(dep 9.24pm) conveying traffic for the Bristol mail. But the most remarkable trains must have been the 9.58am and 5.10pm Selby-Leeds and the 7.20am Leeds-Selby and 4.28pm Leeds-Bridlington which ran via Wetherby and Church Fenton, taking the best part of two hours between Leeds and Selby. Also worth a mention are the unadvertised 6.15am Hull to Thorp Arch ordnance factory (near Wetherby) and 5.28pm return expresses, as shown in the 1955 working timetable. Running via Church Fenton, they were among a number of trains still operating specially for the factory's civilian workforce which came from a wide area The Leeds via

A Hull-Liverpool express rounds the curve out of Selby station past the engine shed on 23rd May, 1959 hauled by B1 4-6-0 No. 61237 *Geoffrey H. Kitson.* The horse box behind the engine was still a feature of passenger trains and working timetables showed which trains were allowed to convey them. Some trains dropped off and picked up horse boxes at stations en-route. *Brian Morrison.*

Above: The six-car Trans-Pennine Class 124 DMUs were the mainstay of Hull-Liverpool services from 1961 until 1979. Their decline was not far away though when this complete 6-car set was photo graphed at Selby on a Liverpool to Hull service in July, 1972. *Stephen Chapman*

Wetherby trains had ceased by 1957 and the Thorp Arch trains by 1958.

A major transformation took place on 2nd January, 1961 when new six-car Inter-City diesel multiple units built at Swindon replaced steam on the Hull-Liverpool expresses. The service was increased to five trains each way on weekdays but none on Sundays. The new trains brought a standard of comfort not seen so far with diesel multiple units, including double glazing in first class and a buffet car famed for its Griddle which served hot snacks like bangers and mash, and the Angus - Aberdeen Angus beef in a toasted bread roll. With them came the Trans-Pennine brand name still used today.

By summer, 1968, the service had increased to eight trains from Liverpool and seven from Hull. The 11.56 Liverpool-Hull was a fast train which did not even stop at Selby, but some others were little more than stopping trains between Selby and Hull. The York-Hull through service had increased to two loco-hauled trains from York and three trains from Hull(two loco-hauled), a so-called improvement trumpeted by BR but in fact a paltry replacement for the direct service via Market Weighton which had been withdrawn in November, 1965. Many were the York-Hull passengers faced with a long wait at Selby for connections in those dark and dismal post-

Beeching years.

The few trains which ran to and from Bridlington via Market Weighton were also withdrawn in 1965 but one train which soldiered on in the diesel era was the evening Hull to Pontefract Baghill, thanks to the continuing demands of the Post Office. By then a DMU set, it ran into the 1970s, Sundays included.

The 1970s saw the expanding motorway network eating away at Trans-Pennine passenger business and by 1976 only around 50 passengers a day were travelling throughout between Hull and Liverpool. The Trans-Pennine DMUs, some having clocked up three million miles, were the worse for wear. By 1975 the buffet cars had been withdrawn because of their condition and trains reduced to five cars with no refreshment facilities. It was time for a rethink and on 14th May, 1979, BR launched a totally re-vamped timetable. Through trains between Hull, Selby and Liverpool were replaced by a Hull-Leeds shuttle worked by the Trans-Pennine units and former Western Region Class 123 Inter-City sets, with just odd trains running between Hull and Manchester Victoria. Decline for Selby was well under way and within little over four years it would be relegated to a relatively minor secondary line junction.

By summer 1984, the service had a rather

different look about it. Eight trains ran from Hull to Leeds and a dozen from Leeds. Three trains ran each way between Hull and Lancaster and one each way between Hull and Carlisle. There was also one train each way between Hull and Bradford Interchange, plus a Hull-Bradford-Manchester Victoria train, and one from Manchester Victoria via Bradford to Selby - a foretaste of things to come. The York-Hull service had been increased to five trains each way, all via Hambleton.

Things had improved a little for Selby by 2001. As well as its rediscovered London trains, it enjoys hourly Hull-Manchester Airport Trans-Pennine Express services operated mostly by air-conditioned 90mph Class 158 multiple units, plus hourly stopping services to and from Manchester Victoria via Bradford. The Hull-York through service has been further enhanced and in 2001 included a train from Middlesbrough but the smaller stations east of Selby - Wressle, Eastrington and Howden - now have a very sparse service indeed.

Of other local services to and from Selby, the Market Weighton line saw a total of five trains each way on weekdays in summer, 1950(there were seven one way and eight the other back in 1910). As well as the few Leeds-Bridlington trains which ran up to closure in 1965, there

were the 9.20am, 2.20pm and 6.20pm Selby-Bridlington all stations and the 7am, 3.45pm and 7pm Bridlington-Selby all stations, plus a Mondays Only 10.5am Holme Moor-Selby. It was a very different matter on summer Saturdays.

A local service plied up and down the Goole branch, consisting in summer 1955 of six trains each way plus one extra on Wednesdays and an additional 1.9pm from Goole on Saturdays. Most trains were worked by push-pull, or "railmotor" as shown in the working timetable, but the 6.55am from Goole and 5.8pm from Selby were conventional hauled trains. The 6.30am Selby-Goole called only at Barlow to set down newspapers while on Saturdays the 5.8pm from Selby ran empty stock. The LNER used Sentinel steam railcars on this service for a time until they were replaced by ex-NER G5 0-4-4Ts and push-pull coaches, latterly 67250 and 67253 which in turn gave way to DMUs in 1957.

The Cawood branch originally had a service of five trains each way, operated by the Manning Wardle 0-6-0ST *Cawood* until taken over by the NER which later used a petrol-electric railcar and a Leyland bus on rail wheels.

With the L&Y and the Great Central enjoying running powers over the NER's line through Goole to Hull and the NER enjoying similar powers through to Doncaster, a range of services

Two trains a day ran direct between Hull and Liverpool Central via Doncaster, Sheffield Victoria, Manchester Central and the Cheshire Lines, and in 1957 they left Goole for Liverpool at 10am and 4.59pm. Here, K3 2-6-0 No. 61816 restarts the morning train from the station in summer, 1960. It is interesting to see how neat the trackside was in those days. *Peter Cookson/N. E. Stead collection.*

operated by those companies eventually linked Goole directly with King's Cross, Manchester and Liverpool. They included The Continental Boat Train run jointly by the NER and L&Y in summer between Liverpool and Hull Riverside to connect with their jointly-operated Hull-Zeebrugge ferry. In the early years of the 20th Century the North Eastern, Lancashire & Yorkshire, London & North Western, Midland and Great Central railways carried thousands of migrants escaping hardship and oppression in Eastern Europe from Hull to Liverpool where they set sail for a new life in the USA. Around five trains a week travelled via Selby and Leeds, Goole and Wakefield or Sheffield depending on which company was operating them.

In summer, 1950, around 20 weekday passenger trains each way traversed all or part of the Staddlethorpe-Thorne Junction line through Goole. The pride of the line was undoubtably the Yorkshire Pullman - through Pullman cars from and to Hull being attached to and detached from the main Leeds-King's Cross train at Doncaster. There were two through trains from Hull to King's Cross and three from King's Cross with an extra on Saturdays, plus one other working of through carriages each way. The line also saw two expresses each way between Hull and Liverpool Central which ran via Doncaster and Sheffield Victoria, plus a through express each way between Hull and Wakefield Kirkgate, the westbound train extended to Manchester on summer Fridays. Just one express ran each way between Hull and Sheffield Midland and the odd express betwee Hull and Doncaster. Stopping trains ran between Hull and Doncaster, Hull and Goole, one each way between Hull and Stainforth & Hatfield and one each way between Hull and Thorne North.

Services remained much the same throughout the 1950s and early 1960s though by 1955 there were a small number of express and stopping trains between Hull and Sheffield Victoria.

By summer, 1968 the London service consisted of four King's Cross to Hull through trains and two from Hull(a third, the 08.55 from Hull ran via Selby.) They included the Hull Pullman which replaced the Yorkshire Pullman through carriages in 1967. The Sheffield Victoria trains had been replaced by six Sheffield Midland-Hull and five Hull-Sheffield Midland trains, one each way extended to and from Chesterfield. The

Liverpool Central and Wakefield trains were no more but during the summer season there were additional Friday night expresses from Hull to Paignton and King's Cross at 22.28 and 23.50 respectively. Notable among stopping trains was the 16.05 Snaith to Hull which started from Snaith on school days and from Goole on other days.

Ten years later the service had increased to around 25 trains each way. Some Hull-King's Cross services had again been running as Hull-Doncaster portions, three coaches hauled by a Class 31 or 37 locomotive, sometimes a Class 47 or Deltic, until the advent of High Speed Trains in the late 1970s. The Hull Pullman made its last run on Friday 5th May, 1978, replaced the following Monday by the Hull Executive, a train consisting of standard air-conditioned Inter-City coaches instead of Pullman cars and destined to become BR's fastest diesel-hauled passenger train when Deltic-hauled. As part of the Trans-Pennine revamp on 14th May, 1979, the Hull Doncaster-Manchester Piccadilly DMU service was increased to three trains each way, becoming loco-hauled in 1984.

By summer, 1984 the line through Goole saw a remarkable array of expresses. For although the Hull-King's Cross trains were reduced to just two each way, Goole also had InterCity trains connecting it directly with London Paddington, Cardiff and Brighton in the shape of the 07.43 Hull-Cardiff, 13.22 Hull-Brighton, 13.55 Cardiff-Hull and the 06.50 Paddington-Hull which reached Goole at 12.15. By 1991, the number of Hull-King's Cross trains was back up to three each way but this was of no use to Goole because from that summer they ceased to call there, BR claiming that the timber platform extensions needed to accommodate the longer trains were not safe to use.

In 2001 the service was composed entirely of Hull-Doncaster/Sheffield express and stopping trains running approximately every half hour.

On the Axholme Joint, a passenger service ran between Goole, Haxey and Fockerby from 1905 until 1933. There were three or four trains each way between Goole and Haxey and two or three each way to and from Fockerby but times and the number of trains varied depending on whether it was a Wednesday, Saturday or any other weekday. For the final three years they were worked by a Sentinel steam railcar owned

Class V3 2-6-2T No. 67640 rolls into Goole station with the Hull portion of the Yorkshire Pullman to King's Cross at 11am on a foggy 7th November, 1961. Goole lost its direct London service in 1991 when British Rail said the timber platform extensions shown here needed major repairs which could not be justified for the number of passengers using the London trains. *David Holmes*

by the Axholme Joint Committee.

The group of lines carrying long-distance expresses just to the west of Selby were those which ran south from York and passed through Church Fenton on their way to Sheffield and Leeds. The Normanton and Sheffield lines parted company at Burton Salmon and it was the Sheffield line through Pontefract - the Swinton & Knottingley - which traditionally carried the bulk of what were termed North East-South West trains, principally Newcastle-Bristol supplemented by a few between varying origins and destinations, such as the York-Bournemouth often with Southern Region green coaches. On weekdays in summer, 1950 and 1955 11 northbound and 9 southbound North East-South West expresses passed Church Fenton and took the S&K. In summer, 1957 the number had increased to 13 northbound and 15 southbound and by 1968 it was back to 12 northbound and 10 southbound. The odd express also ran between York and Sheffield, varying between Midland and Victoria depending on the year. The smaller stations, including Church Fenton, were served mainly by York-Sheffield/Leeds stopping trains.

Among parcels trains which came via the S&K was the 7.40pm from Sheffield Midland. The

1955 working timetable showed it running to Sherburn South Junction from where the engine propelled its single van up to Gascoigne Wood. It then ran light to Milford sidings where it collected the 10.20pm fish to Birmingham.

Services using the Lancashire & Yorkshire main line between York and Manchester Victoria also passed through Church Fenton, taking the Normanton route at Burton Salmon. The premier train of the 1950s was the 10.30am Liverpool Exchange-Newcastle express and 5.10pm return from Newcastle, boasting a dining car, limited to 400 tons, and hauled by one of Liverpool Bank Hall shed's three Jubilees, *Mars, Dauntless* or *Glorious*, or its un-named Patriot No. 45517. By the start of the 1960s it ran only between Liverpool and York. Also class A trains during the 1950s were the unadvertised 6.55am SX Normanton-Thorp Arch which called at Sherburn-in-Elmet, at 7.16, and the 5.32pm return which called there at 6.21.

During the 1960s, the Normanton line passenger service was heavily pruned and by summer, 1968 consisted of just three Manchester Victoria-York DMUs each way with a small number running over shorter distances, plus a seasonal Wakefield-Scarborough train each way and the

02.10 York-Manchester Victoria mail. On 5th January, 1970 the remaining passenger trains were withdrawn, leaving the Burton Salmon-Castleford section of the line to freight, parcels and a few summer seaside excursions.

As the 1960s passed the S&K was hit more and more by mining subsidence and by the 1970s it is fair to say it was probably the worst affected main line in the country. In 1973 BR switched all its North East-South West expresses to the Normanton route. The local York-Sheffield service via the S&K was increased to eight trains each way, but over the years it was whittled down until in 2001 there were just three inconveniently timed northbound trains and two southbound, reduced to two each way on Saturdays. These formed the bulk of the trains serving Sherburn and Ulleskelf.

With the introduction of High Speed Trains in 1981, resignalling and 115mph running were proposed under a £10.4 million upgrade for the whole North East-South West route, including the York-Normanton section, but the plan was short-lived. Newly formed BR Inter-City business management, faced with coach competition, a recession and a serious embankment slip south of Normanton, diverted what they now call Cross-Country trains away from the Normanton line in May, 1984. Many were rerouted via Doncaster, taking advantage of the new Selby diversion and others via the York-Leeds line. The Burton Salmon-Castleford section was again left with only its summer seaside excursions. Passenger trains were completely eliminated at the end of the 1992 summer season with the last run of the Sunday Only Wakefield-Scarborough. Now and then, when there is a blockage between York and Leeds, passenger trains are diverted via Burton Salmon, following the pre-1869 route between the two cities.

Opening of the York-Leeds direct line and Leeds New Station in 1869 cleared the way for the introduction of expresses between Liverpool and York in the late 19th century but for most of the time the bulk of the line's passenger service has run between York or Scarborough and Leeds - in summer, 1957 there were 12 eastbound and 10 westbound trains every weekday with some running to and from Bradford Forster Square. The premier train, however, was the 9.15am Leeds to Glasgow and 4pm return North Briton with one of Neville Hill shed's A3 Pacifics at the head.

LMS Jubilee 4-6-0 No. 5629 *Straits Settlements* makes a stirring sight as it hurries along between York and Church Fenton with a York to Sheffield Midland stopping service in 1947. In 2001, this service often consisted of a one-vehicle railcar. *Ernest Sanderson / Stephen Chapman collection*

Just one Liverpool-Newcastle express in each direction took this route. Other 1950s expresses included two Leeds-Newcastle trains each way, a Bradford Forster Square-Newcastle, the 5.37pm Manchester Exchange-Newcastle and at night the York-Swansea mail. The sparse stopping service consisted of just three or four York-Leeds trains each way plus the 6.40am Leeds-Church Fenton which formed the 7.40 Church Fenton-Wetherby-Leeds.

The 1960s saw dieselisation and rationalisation. The North Briton went over to Type 4 power but loco failures often saw an A1 Pacific substituted; Sulzer Type 2s were tried on the Leeds-Newcastle trains which ended up formed of ordinary Metro-Cammell DMUs equipped with buffet cars. Trains ceased running to and from Bradford Forster Square but the number of Leeds-York local trains was increased while the number of Leeds-York-Scarborough expresses remained about the same. Closure of the Leeds Northern route north of Harrogate in March, 1967 saw all Newcastle-Liverpool trains, four each way, routed via York. By summer, 1968 the overnight mail was running between York and Aberystwyth.

By summer, 1978 the number of Liverpool-Newcastles had increased to five each way plus a Liverpool-Edinburgh during July and August. The North Briton had become history, in its place an 07.30 Leeds-Edinburgh and the mail only

went as far as Shrewsbury; the Leeds-Newcastle DMUs were long gone. The May, 1979 re-vamp of Trans-Pennine services saw a new York-Liverpool loco-hauled service, extended to include Scarborough and North Wales in 1982. These were joined in 1984 by North East-South West InterCity services switched from the York-Normanton route and the York-Leeds line became rather busy to say the least.

In 2002 the line is used by very frequent Class 158 TransPennine multiple units running between Newcastle, Sunderland, Middlesbrough, Scarbrough, York, Manchester Airport, Liverpool and Blackpool, Virgin Cross Country expresses - loco-hauled and HST - hourly York-Manchester Victoria via Bradford trains which form the stopping service, and one GNER early morning Leeds-Aberdeen HST, a remnant of the North Briton.

On summer Saturdays during the 1950s and early 1960s the railway system in this part of the country was inundated with scores of extra trains carrying holidaymakers to and from the Yorkshire coast. They came from all parts of the West Riding, Lancashire, the East and West Midlands and even further afield bringing with them an array of foreign locomotives. Forty-odd years on and looking at the railway today, it is hard to imagine just how hectic it was on a summer Saturday in those days of steam. Every Saturday

Class A3 Pacific No. 60092 *Fairway* **coasts through Church Fenton on the Leeds-York line with the 5.30pm Leeds City to Newcastle at 5.54 on Sunday 8th May, 1960. No. 60092 had earlier double-headed the Newcastle-Manchester Red Bank vans to Leeds with B1 No. 61021** *Reitbok.* *David Holmes.*

An excursion hauled by B16/3 4-6-0 No. 61472 races along the Up Leeds line past Bolton Percy station on 16th September, 1961. The Leeds lines were originally the 1839 York & North Midland route to Normanton, the present Normanton lines and station on the right being added in the early 1900s. The buildings on the left are the original station.
Rebuilds of the original B16/1s , the B16/3s were introduced in 1944. *P. B. Booth / N.E.Stead collection.*

in high summer 1957 a staggering 100 booked additional trains passed over the lines previously mentioned, over half of them funnelling through Selby and no less than 38 taking the Market Weighton line to and from Bridlington, Scarborough and Butlins holiday camp near Filey. Some stopped at Gascoigne Wood to take water or swap their London Midland engines for North Eastern engines. Saturdays would also see extra relief trains, charter excursions and the like. Many trains utilised spare locomotives and coaches stored throughout the winter, and goods engines were pressed into passenger service to meet this seasonal peak in demand. There were just too many summer Saturday trains to mention them individually but practically every route in the district had its share.

In the later 1960s, increasing car ownership, overseas package holidays, Beeching closures and a drive to eliminate spare coaching stock saw a rapid decline in summer Saturday traffic which continued through the 1970s and 1980s. By the mid-1990s such trains had as good as disappeared.

In addition to its railway operations, the L&Y also operated steamer sailings from Goole to Rotterdam, Antwerp, Dunkirk, Hamburg and Copenhagen. By 1950 they were operated by Goole Steam Shipping, part of the Railway Executive(Humber Services), one of the three constituents of Associated Humber Lines.

In the 1950s, services from Goole sailed to Antwerp, Dunkirk, Ghent, Amsterdam, Rotterdam, Copenhagen, Hamburg and Bremen but by then consisted of cargo boats with only limited passenger accommodation. By 1961, the only remaining sailings were to Bremen, from Hamburg, and to and from Copenhagen.

Freight

The driving force for freight in this part of Yorkshire has traditionally come from three sources - long distance traffic between the South, the Midlands and the North, the movement of goods to and from the Humber ports, and the coal industry. From what is about to follow it can be seen that the amount of freight traffic back in the 1950s and early 60s was phenomenal. On top of all those "booked" trains were many, many coal trains and trip workings which were not shown in the working timetables. How we long for such days now as heavy lorries crowd us off the roads while the railway is almost barren of freight.

By and large, only class C and D express freights(fitted with vacuum brake on all or at least 90 per cent of wagons) were allowed on the East Coast main line between Doncaster and York, and many of those were at night. The few exceptions were unfitted or partially fitted trains running between Grimsby, Scunthorpe and the North via Joan Croft Junction which could not avoid the ECML. Even so, some of these were routed via Gascoigne Wood and Church Fenton to avoid as much of the main line as possible.

The winter 1959/1960 working timetable showed around 32 booked northbound trains over the ECML through Selby every 24 hours during the week, and 43 southbound. They consisted mainly of express freights between London or Whitemoor yard(March), York, the North East and Scotland(mainly Niddrie yard) - a number of which advertised guarenteed arrival times. The most outstanding train was the 3.5pm

King's Cross Goods to Niddrie class C, booked for an A4 Pacific and passing Selby at 7.29pm. This train was authorised to run non-stop from King's Cross to York without even stopping for examination. The corresponding southbound train the 6.5pm from Niddrie was booked to pass Selby at 11.8pm and ran to accelerated class C timings.

Other prime freights were the Aberdeen-King's Cross meat trains which passed Selby at 7.10 and 7.57pm, the 7.10 running when required. Also class C trains, they took precedence over all others except ECML passenger trains. In the same league were three fish trains - the 12.30pm and 1.45pm Aberdeen and 9pm York to Kings Cross. The York train had an assured arrival while the Aberdeens took priority like the meat trains. The 2pm and 3.5pm Niddrie-Whitemoor class Cs and 10.5am Niddrie-Whitemoor class F, through Selby at 10.28pm, 12.12am and 7.19pm, carried seed potatoes from Scotland to East Anglia during the season. Local traffic was

The legendary King's Cross to Niddrie express goods coasting through Selby at 7.31pm on 22nd July, 1960. Loading to 1,000 tons, this class C train was so highly ranked that not only did it warrent top link express passenger power, in this case A4 Pacific No. 60028 *Walter K. Wigham*, but the working timetable showed it as "authorised to run non-stop between King's Cross and York without intermediate examination." Lesser freight trains stopped several times en-route so that examiners could check such things as springs, axle boxes and wagon doors. *Robert Anderson.*

A York Dringhouses-Ardsley class H Through Freight headed by B1 4-6-0 No. 61013 *Topi* rolls through Church Fenton on 20th April, 1961. The train has been routed from the Up Leeds to the Up Normanton and will continue via Castleford and the Methley Joint line direct to Ardsley. The old engine shed is clearly visible in the left distance, beyond the bare tree. *Peter Rose*

catered for by the 8.55am Doncaster -York class F, the 4.40am York-Doncaster class H and 6.50pm York-Doncaster class F.

Most of the slower unfitted trains were routed via Askern, Knottingley and Church Fenton, well clear of the East Coast expresses.

With around two dozen booked freights each way per 24 hours in winter 1959/60, traffic heading to and from the S. & K. was varied and fascinating. Most memorable were the vast trains hauling huge quantities of East Midlands iron ore from such places as Storefield and Wellingborough to the North East blast furnaces, hauled as far as York by ex-LMS Beyer-Garratts, Great Central 2-8-0s and BR 9F 2-10-0s - often so grimy it was impossible to read their numbers. A considerable number of mixed freights ran between York and such places as Annesley, Mottram and Woodford Halse on the former Great Central system

Among noteworthy trains were three officially named class Cs. These were the 6.40pm Park Lane(Gateshead) to Washwood Heath - The Birmingham Braked - the 5.30am York Dringhouses to Cardiff - The Welshman - and the 5.55am York Dringhouses to Bristol - The Bristol. All three were booked to stop and attach wagons at Milford. Of other trains, the 8.50pm Birmingham Lawley Street to Dringhouses class C stopped at Milford to detach fitted wagons for Hull which had to be marshalled next to the engine; and the 9.15pm York to Birmingham fish called at Milford to attach vans from Hull.

Besides coal trains, the steady procession of Normanton line freight amounted to 40 Down(northbound) class C to H trains and 30 Up(southbound) class C to H trains per 24 hours in winter 1959/60. They included trains from the yards at Healey Mills Wakefield, Ardsley and Normanton to York, Hull and the North East, and trains from York, Hull and the North East to Normanton, Ardsley and Mirfield as well as trains to and from a variety of places across the Pennines, including Manchester, Liverpool, Birkenhead and Shrewsbury. Notable express

21

A westbound class F unfitted express freight from Hull, probably bound for York, thunders through Staddlethorpe on 13th May, 1953 behind B16/3 4-6-0 No. 61444. *B.G. Tweed / N.E. Stead collection*

workings along this route were the 7.30pm Liverpool Huskisson to Dringhouses, the 1.10am Monday excepted Dringhouses to Walton, the 5pm Sundays excepted Holyhead to York cattle train, and the 8.50pm Hull to Normanton fish.

Local goods trains included the 6.35am Ardsley-Selby, 10.38am Selby-Ardsley and 6.30pm Normanton-Selby class H trains, and the 8.50pm(9.5 on Sats) Selby-Normanton class E. Considering that the traffic from all these latter three routes converged at Burton Salmon, the section from there to Milford was very busy indeed.

The Leeds & Selby carried 17 eastbound and 19 westbound booked freights per 24 hours in winter 1959/60. Besides the Hull-Selby-Normanton/Ardsley and Frodingham-York trains already mentioned, they included trains between Hull and Leeds Neville Hill Sidings and between Hull, York and the North East via Gascoigne Wood and Church Fenton. The line's premier train was the officially named Humber-Clyde, the 6.50pm Hull Outward Yard to Glasgow High Street class C assured arrival service booked to pass through Selby at 7.35pm. Other notable trains were the 1.20pm SX Hull Outward Yard to Leeds City fish, through Selby at 2.1pm, and the 6.25pm Hull Outward Yard to Manchester fish, passing Selby at 7.8pm. The

4.50pm Healey Mills to York Dringhouses class C ran via Selby to pick up wagons between 6.50 and 7.15pm, while the 9.45pm Saturday Hull Outward Yard to Peterborough East Goods class C actually only ran as far as Selby Canal where it arrived at 10.35pm ready to transfer its wagons to the 11.45pm Dringhouses-King's Cross.

On Mondays, Wednesdays and Fridays, an untimed early morning class K pick-up ran from Selby to Hessle Haven, calling when required at Hemingbrough, North Howden and South Eastrington. The return working was shown to depart Hull Outward Yard at 8.50am, calling when required at Williamson's Siding, North Howden, Wressle and Hemingbrough. It was booked to call at Staddlethorpe in both directions. Peckfield Colliery sent two booked but untimed loaded class H coal trains direct to Hull each evening, returning class E empties leaving Hull Outward Yard at 4.50am and 3.15pm.

The Doncaster-Goole-Staddlethorpe line carried 43 Up(southbound) and 35 Down(northbound) freights each 24 hours, which when put with the Hull-Selby line trains already referred to demonstrates the scale of the traffic generated by Hull Docks in those days. Nearly half of all the trains were daytime class H mineral trains carrying shipping coal from such mining centres as Staveley Central, Mansfield, Wath, Frickley and Colwick, and they included trains from Cudworth and Bullcroft which ran over the Hull & Barnsley Railway until that line's closure to through traffic in 1958.

Class C express freights, many during the night, passed through Goole on their way to Hull from King's Cross, Ancoates(Manchester) and Woodford Halse, and from Hull to Whitemoor and East Goods. From late afternoon to mid evening on a weekday the patient observer at Goole could revel in a procession of five fish trains heading away from Hull, their cargoes bound for chippies far away. First through at 4.5pm was the 3.30 to East Goods, then at 4.45 the 4.10 to Plymouth, after a gap the next at 6.40pm was the 6.5 to Banbury, followed at 7.26 by the 6.55 to King's Cross which was allowed just 10 minutes from Staddlethorpe to Thorne Junction, and finally at 8.18, the 7.42 Hull to Guide Bridge. Class D trains came through from Colwick, Sheffield, Annesley and Doncaster, and from Hull to Aintree and Mottram. Other freights came from Healey Mills, Bradford, Whitemoor, Aintree, Woodford Halse, Dewsnap, Manchester Brewery Sidings and ran to Crewe, Whitemoor, Annesley, Rose Grove, Manchester Oldham Road, Frodingham and Bradford Adolphus Street. Local workings included an untimed morning class K trip from Goole to Saltmarshe which shunted at Skelton Bridge siding when required.

The heavy freight traffic for which the 11-mile branch to Selby was built for may not have materialised but it did have a couple of trains each way. In winter 1959/60, the day's first working was the 6am Goole to Selby engine and brake van which then formed the 8am class K pick-up from Selby, calling at Barlow to detach wagons and shunt the ordnance depot and railway tip as required before also calling when required at Drax Hales, Newland Siding, Airmyn & Rawcliffe and Oak Hill. No time was booked for the next working to Selby which called at Airmyn & Rawcliffe, Newland Siding, Drax Hales, Barlow and Barlow Tip when required. This then returned as the 12.30pm Selby to Goole, booked to call only at Barlow. The day's final train was the 6.15pm(6.25 on Saturday) class D from Goole.

At that time, the whole of the Axholme Joint was served by a class K pick-up due away from Goole Sidings at 8.20am before spending the day meandering around the system, going first to Reedness Junction, then Fockerby, Epworth and

It is Goole station at 11.26am on 7th November, 1961 and Class 04/8 2-8-0 No. 63893 is heaving a heavy class H coal train on its way to Hull. The carriage sidings housing DMUs on the right have long since been abandoned and built over. *David Holmes*

The Axholme Joint pick-up spent most of the day meandering around the system to Haxey, Hatfield Moor and Fockerby. This is it at Hatfield Moor in the mid-1950s being worked by Ivatt Class 2 2-6-0 No. 46436. *G. Oates*

finally Hatfield Moor as required.

The L&Y line from Goole to Pontefract and Wakefield or Leeds was just as busy as the other main lines with between 25 and 30 booked freights each way per 24 hours. Much of the traffic consisted of coal trains from various collieries to Goole Docks for shipping, or to the yards at Crofton, Wakefield, Normanton and Healey Mills with returning empties. In the midst of all these slow moving mineral trains ran a number of express freights: the 9pm Hull to Aintree class D, the 5pm Goole Sidings to Hunslet class D, the 10.55pm Brewery Sidings to Goole Beverley Sidings class D, the 10.30pm Bradford to Hull class E, 7.55pm Aintree to Hull class E, the 11.20pm Hull to Bradford Adolphus Street class E, and the 10.15pm Healey Mills to Hull class E. Local class K trips included the 6.5am Goole Sidings to Knottingley and the 11am Knottingley to Goole Beverley Sidings, and the 6pm Wakefield Whithams Sidings to Goole. In addition to these, the 1.35pm Goole to Turners Lane class H shunted at Snaith when required while looped to let other trains pass.

Trip workings centred on Gascoigne Wood marshalling yard until it closed in 1959 served the collieries in the Castleford and Pontefract areas, worked by Selby engines, mostly Q6 0-8-0s. The

new Selby coalfield with its huge rail loading point at Gascoigne Wood added fresh impetus to coal workings which had been revolutionised in the 1960s and 70s by the introduction of Merry-go-Round working in which block 1,000-ton trains ran direct between pits and the big Aire Valley power stations at Ferrybridge, Eggborough and Drax, discharging their loads at the power stations without stopping. In 1989 Gascoigne Wood was despatching 95 loaded MGR trains a week to the Aire Valley power stations, well short of its 50 a day capacity but impressive all the same.

Most other forms of freight declined sharply from the 1960s onwards: local depots were closing, Hull and Goole docks were in sharp decline and traffic was handed to road hauliers on a plate. Coal shipments through Hull had ceased by the early 1970s and through Goole not long after; hardly any fish had been carried by rail since the late 1960s. Freight along the Hull and Goole lines was reduced to just a handful of trains. By 1973 the Hensall-Goole section of the once bustling Knottingley-Goole line had no booked freight traffic and was ultimately reduced to single track.

But new freight traffic was won - oil trains from Immingham refineries to a terminal at Hunslet East, Leeds, reached via Joan Croft and

Selby, and block trains carrying stone from Rylstone(near Skipton) to Hull and, in the 1970s, Goole. A new freight terminal on the site of the closed Selby sugar factory and the Plasmor building blocks railhead at Heck have kept freight alive on the Selby-Doncaster line.

The 1990s saw a modest revival of Hull and Goole docks. Helped by a £22 million investment package from Associated British Ports, Goole has become a thriving port again with steel and containerised freight generating most of the rail traffic. Coal trains run again on the Doncaster and Selby-Hull lines - only this time they are carrying imported coal, shipped in through Hull. In 2001 around 70 booked freights still ran over that busy Milford-Burton Salmon stretch every 24 hours - not exceptional in the late 1950s but a hell of a lot by today's standards.

All change

No sooner had the Leeds & Selby opened than it became the first railway in Yorkshire to close, a victim of railway magnate George Hudson's ruthless pursuit of his ambitions. In November, 1840 Hudson's YNMR took a 31-year lease on the Leeds & Selby and rerouted all its passengers via Milford and the North Midland Railway, leaving the Gascoigne Wood-Leeds section with no passenger trains at all. Instead of arriving at Marsh Lane station in Leeds, passengers went to the NMR's Hunslet Lane terminus, many having to change into York-Leeds trains at Milford where a new station replaced the one at York Junction. Through freight was similarly diverted in 1848, leaving the L&S with only trip workings serving local collieries. Hudson's route was 4.5 miles longer but it did at least enable passengers and freight to connect with other lines rather than just terminate at the isolated Marsh Lane. A local passenger service recommenced in 1850 when York Junction station reopened as Old Junction. That was how things remained until 1869 when the NER opened the direct York-Leeds line and Leeds-Hull trains were restored to the L&S route. From then on the local railway network enjoyed stability and continued to prosper.

But difficulties in the wake of the first world war and the spread of motor buses brought the need for economies early in the 20th century. These began in a small way at first. Old Junction station(renamed Milford Old Junction in 1867 and Gascoigne Wood in 1879) was closed in 1902, and Milford station in 1904. In 1930 the LNER axed the Cawood passenger service and in 1933 marked its takeover of the Axholme Joint by withdrawing that line's passenger trains on 17th July. That same year it also introduced colour light signalling between Goole and Saltmarshe,

Among the economies which the LNER, and the Axholme Joint, tried in an attempt to make branch line services less uneconomic were the Sentinel steam railcars. No. 2136, appropriately named _Hope_, stands in the bay platform at Selby with a Goole branch service in summer, 1947. The attempt was in vain and this was the only such railcar to survive into British Railways ownership following nationalization in 1948. _Neville Stead collection._

The Cawood passenger service was an early casualty in the face of economic depression and more convenient buses, being withdrawn by the LNER on 1st January, 1930. This was the disused passenger station some 30 years later, shortly before goods traffic was withdrawn. *N. E. Stead collection.*

abolishing signal boxes at each end of Goole bridge and one in Goole.

Nationalization in 1948 did not halt the creeping tide of cutbacks and in 1954 the local passenger service between Selby and Market Weighton became the next victim. The final rundown of the Axholme Joint began on 1st February, 1956 when BR closed the line completely beyond Epworth. The Hatfield Moor branch went in 1963 and the remaining section between Marshland Junction, Epworth and Fockerby in April, 1965. The track was left in situ for the Central Electricity Generating Board which was proposing a new power station along the line at Belton, but it never materialised and it was finally lifted in 1972.

Most intermediate stations on the Doncaster-York line were some distance from the villages they served and were early casualties of the BR era. Naburn and Escrick closed to passengers and Moss to all traffic on 8th June, 1953, Heck, Balne and Riccall to passengers on 15th September, 1958, and Temple Hirst to passengers on 6th March, 1961. Remaining goods facilities followed during the 1960s.

In 1958, a start was made on reconstructing bridges between Selby and York in readiness for electrification of the East Coast main line. Alas, BR then decided that the West Coast route should take priority and the electrification was shelved, destined not to restart until the 1980s.

Less positive things were happening around Selby. The decline in coal exported through Hull during the second half of the 1950s led to the closure of Gascoigne Wood marshalling yard in November, 1959, and the Selby engine shed which provided its power. For the next 20 years or so the yard would only be used for wagon storage and engineers' traffic.

The 1960s dawned with the Cawood branch shutting completely on 2nd May, 1960. Then came the Beeching years when lines and stations were closed one after the other and surviving services modified. Major casualties in 1964 were the Church Fenton-Wetherby line closing to passengers on 6th January, and the Selby-Goole line to passengers in June. The Selby-Goole line closed completely between Barlow and Goole on 7th December, but the Brayton Junction-Barlow section was retained to serve the railway tip until October, 1984, Brayton Junction still being in situ in 2002. The Thorpe Willoughby-Brayton section had closed in 1945, superseded by the Selby Canal-West curve which was perfectly able to carry any traffic that might run between Gascoigne Wood and Goole. In 1969 the Goole line was temporarily reinstated between Barlow

1959 CDS GASWOOD
BARLOW

and Drax for the delivery of materials during construction of Drax power station.

June, 1965 saw complete closure of the Selby-Market Weighton line and diversion or withdrawal of summer Saturday traffic. Anticipating the closure, the Derwent Valley Light Railway saw no purpose in retaining a through route and closed the Cliffe Common end of its line in 1964.

The next bit of railway to disappear was the remaining Church Fenton-Tadcaster portion of the Wetherby branch from which goods services were axed on 30th November, 1966.

The 1960s were also an era of modernisation and since then signalling throughout the whole area has been progressively modernised - to the point that by the late 1990s the only surviving semaphores were at Gilberdyke, as Staddlethorpe had been renamed in 1974.

Generally, the post-Beeching years of the late 1960s and early 1970s presented a desolate scene with surviving local passenger services often sparse, running at inconvenient times and by roundabout routes. They were being deserted by commuters as car ownership grew while on the roads traffic congestion was being invented. In 1972, however, BR tried to stem the loss with a major promotion of its local services in the West Riding, each route being given its own brand name. The campaign worked and an annual five per cent loss in passengers was turned round into a five per cent gain. But more was to follow.

On 1st January, 1976 the West Yorkshire County Council through its Passenger Transport Executive took financial responsibility for the county's public transport with the aim of securing the future of those local rail services that remained. Initially it supported the Leeds-Micklefield service but from 1978 it began supporting most local services in the county, including the Knottingley-Leeds route.

Outside West Yorkshire, however, things were not so rosy. Trains between Knottingley and Goole were steadily eroded until only two from Leeds and three from Goole remain in 2002. Only the operational convenience of Selby and York as turnback points for local trains east of Leeds has ensured that local services continue to run beyond Micklefield at hourly intervals. The York-Sheffield local service through Church Fenton is nowadays little better than that between Knottingley and Goole. Yet as it declined,

Sherburn-in-Elmet station actually reopened in 1984 - but not far away, disaster loomed.

Faced with a £2 million repair bill for Goole bridge after years of being repeatedly hit and damaged by ships, British Rail proposed closure of the Goole-Gilberdyke line and Saltmarshe station. All through traffic was to be diverted via Selby with a local service running only between Goole and Doncaster, and buses between Goole and Hull. Goole station would be resited so as to abolish the busy Boothferry Road level crossing while diversion of through services via Selby would justify retention of double track between Selby and Temple Hirst following opening of the Selby Diversion.

The closure proposal caused an outcry and was withdrawn a year later after a cash injection by Humberside County Council enabled the work to go ahead. The repairs were almost complete when, on 23rd November, 1988 a 3,500-ton Swedish cargo vessel rammed one of the bridge's fixed spans, pushing the structure 30ft out of alignment and raising the spectre of closure yet again. After deliberating for three months, BR stated that it would repair the bridge after local councils agreed to contribute towards insurance against ship strikes. By the time these latest repairs were completed in October, 1989, the line and its bridge had been closed for just short of a a year.

Despite many cutbacks in the rail system and thanks to the Selby coal mine and the big three power stations, the railways around Selby and Goole have managed to retain some level of interest, being one of the few places on Britain's rail network to still carry considerable freight traffic. Church Fenton provides the observer with plenty of activity while every weekday enthusiasts gather on the overbridge at the south end of Milford yards watching a continuous procession of freight movements.

From 29th October, 2001, the Wakefield-Goole line east of the junction with the Drax power station branch became effectively disused. On that day, the train operator Arriva suspended all Leeds-Goole trains, plus the Saturday York-Sheffield local service, and replaced them with buses because it was short of train drivers. The situation was expected to last at least until early 2002.

Left: Photographed from a Selby-York DMU, BR Standard Britannia class Pacific No. 70008 *Black Prince* heads a southbound class C fitted freight past the exit from the Up Goods Independent between Escrick and Riccall. on 27th March, 1963. The Up and Down Independent lines were added in 1942 to cope with wartime traffic and at each end included air raid precaution signal boxes of wartime austerity construction - rectangular brick buildings with flat concrete roofs and metal window frames. The loops were abandoned during resignalling in 1966/67.
Peter Rose.

Following the 1966/67 modernisation, the line speed between Selby and York was 90mph.
Signalling between Barlby North and York was Track Circuit Block under the control of York signal box, the remaining intermediate boxes at Escrick South, Riccall North and Riccall South having been abolished along with the gate boxes at Riccall York Road and Turnhead. Level crossings were converted to automatic half barriers.

SELBY & THE EAST COAST MAIN LINE

A sight easily seen from trains on the York-Selby line was the clay pit at Escrick where a 2ft gauge railway carried clay to Henry Oakland's tile works. A permanent section of the railway used heavy flat bottom rail and included a passing loop.It was all replaced by dump trucks in 1979.
Here, one of the works' six Motorail locos, No. 9655, built 1951, stands with a train of skips on 20th June, 1979.
Adrian Booth

Above: Class A1 4-6-2 No. 60114 *W. P. Allen* heads a southbound Class D(vacuum brake operating on at least 90 per cent of the train) express goods past semaphore signals near Riccall. The semaphores were replaced by colour lights during the 1966/67 resignalling. Since closing in 1983 this section of the East Coast main line has been swallowed up by the A19 Riccall by-pass. *G. W. Sharpe collection*

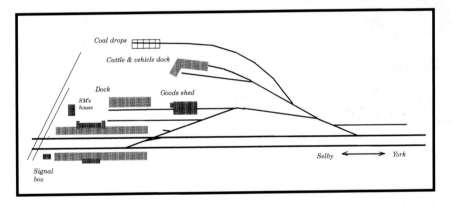

Above The layout at Riccall in 1920. *Not to scale*

The 1956 Railway Clearing House Stations Handbook stated that Riccall goods yard was able to handle a full range of traffic including vehicles and livestock, and was equipped with a 1.5 ton yard crane. The yard was controlled by a three-lever ground frame on the Down side. Reduced to a public delivery siding in 1958, it closed altogether in July, 1964.

A tragic accident took place at Riccall York Road level crossing on 16th July, 1952, partly due to a peculiarity of the signalling controlled by the gatebox there. The one lever controlled both Up and Down home signals protecting the crossing.
With Riccall South having accepted an Up freight from Riccall North, the York Road gateman pulled off the home lever, the Up distant, and closed the gates.
A Down express was then accepted by Riccall North and the gateman pulled off his Down distant. Then he became involved in conversation with a pedestrian over cricket scores, by which time the freight was passing over the crossing and a car had arrived from the Selby direction.
Anxious to let the car pass, the gateman put back the signals and opened the gates. He had forgotten about the express which smashed through the gates, killing the occupants of the car as they crossed.
After this, the Down detonators which had been operated by a lever, were put onto a stirrup pull handle, making the lever available to enable separate levers for the Up and Down home signals.

Above: LNER A4 Pacific No. 20 *Guillemot* heads a York-bound class D freight away from Selby and past Barlby North signal box in 1947. The British Oil & Cake Mills sidings are on the right. The train is just approaching the connections for the intriguingly named Powder Magazine Siding which were controlled by a ground frame. A little further north is Osgodby Siding, a public coal siding also controlled by a ground frame since 1935 when the signal box was abolished.

The Up Distants on the battery of semaphore signals could not be pulled off unless there was a clear road through to Selby South as Selby North could not stop trains at its home signals because they would be standing on the bridge. *This and the picture below: Ernest Sanderson / S. Chapman collection.*

Below: With the huge BOCM mills on each side, 9F 2-10-0 No. 92187 and its class D freight wait on the Down Slow for the Deltic-hauled Flying Scotsman to overtake sometime around 1963. The picture was taken from Barlby level crossing which connects two parts of the BOCM mills.

Left: The last Sentinel vertical boilered steam loco in North Eastern Region capital stock was Selby's Y1 No. 68150, pictured shunting at the BOCM sidings on 22nd August, 1958. No. 68150 was withdrawn on 4th May, 1959. Sentinel steam locos lasted in departmental use until the 1960s.
Neville Stead

Selby private sidings listed by the 1956 Railway Clearing House Handbook of Stations

Bell, Berry & Co.
British Oil & Cake Mills
British Sugar Corporation
Dent's Siding
E.M. Fawcett's Siding
Fletcher's Siding
Kirby's(Selby) Ltd., Flour Mills
North Eastern Gas Board
War Department, Henwick Hall
Yorkshire Dyeware Co.

By 1973, two concerns in Selby still had their own locomotives. BOCM had Hibberd 4 wheel petrol mechanical loco 2896, built in 1944, and a 4-wheel road/rail loco built by Strachan & Henshaw Ltd. of Bristol in 1966. In the early 1970s, Fowler 4200003 was transferred from the company's Stoneferry works in Hull to replace the Hibberd as working loco. In 2001 the fleet consisted of a Unimog road/rail vehicle added in 1982 as well as the Fowler and the S&H road/railer.

The British Sugar Corporation's refinery was the other remaining user of industrial locos with a Ruston & Hornsby 0-4-0 diesel mechanical loco built in 1953 and Barclay 0-4-0ST No. 1862, built in 1925.The steam loco had gone by 1975.

The sugar refinery closed in 1981 and by 1984 the site was converted into a rail freight terminal by Selby Storage which in 2001 still used a Ruston 0-4-0 diesel as well as a Rolls Royce 0-6-0.

Right: Some Selby firms had their own shunting locos, and this has to be the best known of them. BOCM's green-liveried Fowler 0-4-0 diesel No. 4200003, built 1946, has been parked in full view of the main running lines in the sidings on the Up side at Barlby for many years. Nowadays a road/rail tractor shunts the strictly internal system but in 2001 the Fowler, seen here on 26th August, 1978, was still available to deputise.
Adrian Booth.

Left: The bridge operator's view of Selby station on 24th May, 1961 as an English Electric Type 4 rattles across with a Down express. The original Leeds & Selby station is on the left and Selby North signal box on the right. *Peter Rose.*

The Railway Magazine, October, 1955, stated: "Selby swing bridge is operated from a small cabin on top of the bridge, but the control gear has to be released by levers forming part of the frame in Selby North signal box. These levers are in turn released by Selby South box. This gives an adequate margin of protection for all Down trains."

Below: With the swing bridge control cabin aloft, York's WD 2-8-0 No. 90078 hauls a pick-up goods over the River Ouse and into Selby station on 23rd March, 1963. *Peter Rose.*

Above: On 6th July, 1964 Class 01 2-8-0 No. 63773 passes Selby North signal box as it comes off the bridge with a southbound class 7 unfitted express goods. The present swing bridge replaced the Bascule lifting bridge in 1891. For many years it carried all four tracks which were 'gauntleted' or interlaced, the Down lines having crossing vees at the north end and point blades at the south. By 1960, the lines had been reduced to two, the slow lines joining the main lines north and south of the bridge by conventional points. *D.P. Leckonby.*

Below: A4 Pacific No. 60017 *Silver Fox*, complete with its burnished fox on the boiler side, makes a splendid sight for the waiting enthusiasts as it takes the Up Main through Selby station with the southbound Anglo-Scottish Car Carrier at 4.46pm on 9th June, 1960. *Robert Anderson.*

Above: A priceless scene which sums up the very human character of the old steam-worked railway. The driver of V2 2-6-2 No. 60872 *King's Own Yorkshire Light Infantry* awaits the right away with a train to York on 28th March, 1959. The permanent speed restriction board beyond the water crane states a maximum speed of 40mph over the bridge. *Neville Stead.*

Below: Working the very traffic it was built for, well groomed pioneer V2 No. 60800 *Green Arrow* passes through the station on caution with the 12.55am Inverkeithing to King's Cross class C fully fitted express goods at 10.30am on 22nd July, 1960. *Robert Anderson*

Above: Towards the lower end of the spectrum of freight trains which passed through Selby in the days of steam, Class 02 2-8-0 No. 63959 climbs the 1 in 255 away from the bridge with a class H unfitted Through Freight, believed to be the 5.40am Darlington Croft Yard to Scunthorpe, at 12.25pm on 22nd July, 1960. *Robert Anderson.*

Below: A the top end of the spectrum of passenger trains that passed through Selby. Gleaming A4 Pacific No. 60013 *Dominion of New Zealand* accelerates effortlessly southwards with the 5pm Newcastle to King's Cross at 6.48 on 9th June, 1960. *Robert Anderson*

Above: Definitely not holiday weather! The rain and grimy A3 Pacific No. 60053 *Sansovino* make for a gloomy scene as the Scarborough Flyer approaches from the south at 2.56pm on Friday 22nd July, 1960. This Fridays Only train was much more tightly timed than the Saturday version. In the right background, a K1 2-6-0 waits with a Through Freight on the goods line from Selby West. The well stocked goods yard is on the left of the picture. *Robert Anderson.*

Below: One of the famous trains to pass through Selby was the Tees-Tyne Pullman, seen here being whisked on its way from Newcastle to King's Cross by A4 No. 60010 *Dominion of Canada* before the rain on 22nd July, 1960..

By this time, this train was booked for a Type 4 diesel but as was often the case, no diesel was available. The working timetable stated that the maximum load for this train should be 315 tons but on this day the load was 10 Pullman cars - nearer 400 tons. It was booked to pass Selby at 11.4 and a half and that is exactly what it did despite the heavier load. At this time East Coast main line steam locos were still kept in good condition and morale was still high among engine crews. *Robert Anderson*

Above: The scene looking south from Selby station has changed a lot since May, 1952 when B16/3 4-6-0 No. 61449 was caught heading north with a class F goods. The gantry of semaphore signals is long gone and so is the original North Eastern Railway nameboard on the right. *B. G. Tweed / N.E.Stead collection.*

Below: It is 1969, *Flying Scotsman* is the only steam locomotive allowed to run on BR standard gauge metals and rationalisation is under way at Selby. At 15.03 on 26th March, the preserved A3 Pacific passes through with the return leg of a Doncaster-Newcastle test run following overhaul at the Hunslet Engine Co.'s works in Leeds.

The goods line to Selby West has just been lifted along with track in the Down side bay platform but the goods yard still has life in it. The line of cable drums may be for resignalling between Selby and Shaftholme Junction. *Robert Anderson.*

SHORT MEMORIES

January, 1954: The Gascoigne Wood-Milford curve's only booked passenger trains are the 8.40pm Hull-Pontefract and the Sunday 3.40pm Wakefield-Selby-York.

October, 1954: Selby D20 4-4-0 62374 is withdrawn. J39 0-6-0 64904 is transferred to Selby.

3.9.55: D20 62381 and Ivatt 2-6-0 43052 head the 11.35am SO Filey Holiday Camp-Leeds. 62349 and 43098 work this train on the 17th.

The 1956 Stations Handbook showed Selby as equipped to handle the full range of goods traffic, including vehicles, machines on wheels and livestock. The fixed yard crane was of 5 tons capacity.

Above: This Heath Robinson contraption on the Down Main in Selby station in the early 1950s looks to be some kind of hand operated track recording apparatus, possibly a prototype to test equipment for the Matisa track recording trolleys which the North Eastern Region was about to pioneer.
The bowler hatted gentleman on the left appears to be the local permanent way inspector, gauge in hand, while on the right is a young civil engineer by the name of Alan Blower. *Ernest Sanderson.*

Below: Wearing pilot headlamps and shunting Selby goods yard on 22nd May, 1959 was Class J50/3 0-6-0T No. 68948, recently transferred to Selby. The engine is still wearing the 51L shedplate of its previous home, Thornaby. *Brian Morrison.*

Right: This picture may not be technically brilliant but what a classic North Eastern scene. LNER D20 (NER class R) 4-4-0 No. 1234, in original unrebuilt form, steams out of the station and under the NER slotted signals at Selby South with a 1930s local passenger train. No. 1234's brass safety valve cover has gone missing. Built at Gateshead in 1907, it was scrapped in May, 1943. *Ernest Sanderson/Stephen Chapman collection*

In 1950 the train fare from Selby to London was 35s 6d third class(177.5p) and 59s 3d first class(£296p.) A Monthly Return was 47s 8d third class and the princely sum of 71s 6d(357.5p) first class.

Below: The Up Talisman hauled by A2 Pacific No. 60539 *Bronzino* comes under the signal gantry at Selby South on 23rd May, 1959, by which time the old NER signals had been replaced with the standard upper quadrant type. The third coach is passing Selby South signal box, the goods yard is through the bridge on the right and the engine shed on the left. *Brian Morrison.*

Above: TheTalisman from King's Cross to Edinburgh with A4 No. 60025 *Falcon* in charge approaches Selby South on the same day as the previous photograph. Selby Canal yard is on the right and the gas works on the left. *Brian Morrison.*

Below: On 23rd May, 1959 K1 2-6-0 No. 62056 of York shed starts away from the Down Goods line alongside Canal yard with a class F freight conveying a good head of Presflo bulk powder wagons for the north. In the far distance is Selby Canal Junction where the curve round to Selby West diverges, enabling trains from the south to run in the direction of Gascoigne Wood. *Brian Morrison.*

SHORT MEMORIES

Sept., 1955: Selby's Y3 Sentinel 68158 is withdrawn and G5 0-4-4T 67273 moves to Selby. At Goole, L&Y 0-6-0 52331 is withdrawn while 52154 and WD 2-8-0 90260 are transferred there.

Sept., 1957: A new named express, The Fair Maid, starts running through Selby with the new East Coast main line timetable.

Sept., 1958: D49 4-4-0 62730 *Berkshire* transferred to Selby.

Spring, 1959: Ivatt 2-6-0s 43054/7/71, J50 0-6-0T 68948 and T1 4-8-0T 69910 transferred to Selby.

July, 1959: The peak summer timetable features a Selby to Whitby through train, usually formed of an 8-car DMU. Goole's 2-6-4T 42553 is sent away to help with extra trains between Malton and Whitby.

19 & 20.5.60: A3 60082 *Neil Gow* brings the 9am Hull-Liverpool into Selby. No. 60088 *Book Law* works the same train on the 26th.

May, 1960: The 7.30am Hull-York freight, normally a B16 or V2, is Pacific-hauled on several days - A3 60053 *Sansovino* on the 2nd, A1 60140 *Balmoral* on the 12th and 13th, A2/3 60518 *Tehran* on the 14th, A3 60076 *Galopin* on the 15th.

Above: Selby's own J77 0-6-0T No. 68406 was on pilot duty at Canal Yard on this particular drizzly mid-1950s day. Introduced in 1899 under the direction of NER chief mechanical engineer Wilson Worsdell, these engines were rebuilds of 0-4-4Ts dating from the 1870s. The rounded cab shows that 68406 was one of a batch rebuilt at York Queen Street works.
Ernest Sanderson / Stephen Chapman collection.

The January 1969 Eastern Region Sectional Appendix showed the 14-mile main line from Shaftholme Junction to Selby North as signalled by Absolute Block on main and Slow lines with Permissive Block on Goods lines.

Intermediate block post signal boxes were at Moss(2 miles 1275yds north of Shaftholme Jn.), Balne(2 miles 1593yds from Moss), Temple Hirst(3 miles 1544yds from Balne), Henwick Hall(2 miles 809yds from Temple Hirst), Brayton(1347yds from Henwick Hall), Selby Canal(1032yds from Brayton), Selby South(946yds from Canal), and Selby North(423yds from Selby South.)

The maximum permissible speed on main lines was 90mph, 60mph on Slow lines and 40mph on Goods lines.

Additional running lines were two Up and Down Goods lines in each direction between Selby Canal and Selby South, Up and Down Slow (platform) lines between Selby South and North(Permissive Block in force on the Up platform line for trains conveying passengers.)

Heck signal box was abolished in 1967. Resignalling completed in 1970 saw Henwick Hall, Balne and Moss signal boxes reduced to gate boxes and Temple Hirst box abolished. In 1973 the line was brought under the control of Selby West and Shaftholme Junction boxes with Track Circuit Block signalling; Brayton box was reduced to a gatebox but still kept the Staff for the single track to Barlow. All signalling in the Selby area was brought under Selby West with Selby Canal, South and Barlby North boxes also abolished. From October, 1980 the whole line as far north as Henwick Hall came under the new Doncaster power box and Shaftholme Junction box was abolished. Brayton gatebox was abolished in 1988. Moss, Balne and Henwick Hall gateboxes remained operative in 2000.

Above: Class A4 Pacific No. 60034 *Lord Farringdon* makes a splendid sight as it forges past Brayton with a northbound express on a wild and breezy day in the early 1960s. Above the fourth coach are the splitting signals controlling the junction with the Goole branch.

Below: Another classic 1960s scene - the daily block cement train which ran from Cliffe in Kent, to Uddingston, near Glasgow, and brought Southern Region diesel power through Selby. No. D6575 leads the pair of Birmingham/Sulzer Type 3 locos which will work the train as far as York. Another classic of the time, a Ford Thames Trader lorry loaded with straw, waits at the crossing alongside Brayton signal box. Brayton box was built to control the junction with the Goole branch and was equipped with no less than 41 levers, a good few of them remaining spare.
Both Ernest Sanderson/Stephen Chapman collection.

The late Sydney Martin grew up in a railway cottage alongside the Selby-Doncaster line at Temple Hirst and started his railway career at Selby New Yard in 1935.

"Selby was a busy railway centre. There was an inspector and shunt staff in the yard, a shedmaster in charge of the locomotives. Signal boxes had one or two signalmen in them plus a book lad. The station had the station master, three inspectors, one station foreman and two shunters plus porters and guards, both passenger and goods. The telegraph office had a chief clerk with clerical staff.

"There was a fine refreshment room of the old, solid type for many passengers had to change trains at Selby

"Three Up sidings held goods trains for faster trains to pass and there was a Down Independent from Canal to Barlby Junction. The tracks from Hull ran alongside the York lines up to the swing bridge.

"Ships on the River Ouse frequently required the bridge to be opened which meant delay to trains as river traffic always had priority.

"As a schoolboy I travelled to Selby daily from Temple Hirst where my father was a signalman. I remember the pick-up goods which ran from Selby to Moss where it turned back because beyond there, at Shaftholme Junction, it was the Great Northern Railway. The pick-up often had 50 wagons when going outwards, and many when returning in the afternoon. Those busy days of country stations are now gone.

"Temple Hirst had a station master, two adult porters, a lad porter, a clerk(two in busy times such as when the pea special came to take wagons of peas to Selby each day), three signalmen, five plate-layers of which I was one once. Two lattice signal posts were said to have dated from the 1870s. Now all gone, no station there.

"The river bridge at Temple Hirst has bullet holes in it from the rifles of soldiers who guarded it in the first world war. There was a large military hut by the railway where they lived. They had been drinking, at the Sloop Inn I think.

"Heck had a long siding on the Up side where freight trains were shunted to let other trains pass A lot of sand traffic came from Heck on the pick-up. The Knottingley & Goole Canal which passes under the railway just south of the station was very busy; the Hull & Barnsley Railway passed over the main line just north of the station.

"A nasty accident happened at Heck in the 1920s. A Down goods train in the early hours had to be shunted to the Up line for a fast train to pass. The signalman pulled one lever too many and the goods came back at a good pace into the sidings, upturned the coal wagons and the long bogie guard's van ran over the wheels into the station master's bedroom.

"Balne was a quiet station with just the station master and a porter.

"During the second world war, Burn aerodrome had bombers and on Friday, 29th January, 1943 one crashed, killing some platelayers in their hut at meal time. When this large aerodrome was built, emergency signals were installed on the line to protect trains from low flying aircraft. After the war, it was a collecting point for vehicles from the battlefields which came by rail to Henwick Hall sidings to be unloaded at the Small Dock end. Every kind of army vehicle could be seen in long rows.

"There were many crossing keepers along the Selby-Doncaster line, platelayers wives who opened the gates for carts.

"My brother-in-law was permanent way inspector and had charge of the main line from Shaftholme Junction to Chaloner's Whin Junction. He was unfortunately killed by an express along with a ganger while examining the points at Joan Croft Junction.

"Travelling to school one morning, there had been a derailment at Selby Canal box. Our train was sent on to the Goole line at Brayton Junction, to the East box, then along to Thorpe Gates and into Selby from the Leeds direction. That bit of 1912 railway never carried passenger trains, it was built for coal traffic from Gascoigne Wood to Goole and was never successful. I travelled it in a passenger train, over a bridge at Brayton village. It's now all gone, houses standing there.

"There was a small goods yard at Thorpe Gates, and at Henwick Hall where a porter was stationed to deal with the farmers.

"I worked at Gascoigne Wood yard for a short time. Railway cottages stood by the offices along side the line from Sherburn. Inspectors and shunt staff at Gascoigne Wood all lived in that area, as did the guards. A hump shunting engine was in use and there was a signal box at the east end - Hagg Lane.

"Selby BOCM, then Selby OCO, had two trains in each day. The sidings were on both sides of the main lines. They were taken over by the LNER to maintain and I was graded ganger in charge. Now there are no connections with the main line.

" My brother started work on the railway at the age of 14 as a lad porter at Heck. Then he went to work as a book lad in the Selby signal boxes. He had a friend in the telegraph office and they made a wooden telegraph instrument to practice sending messages on the "sounder" needle instrument. That was the enthusiasm of the staff in those days.

Above: Heck will be remembered for the awful tragedy which occurred on 21st February, 2001 when a Newcastle-London express collided head-on with a northbound coal train after being derailed by a Landrover which had crashed on to the main line from the motorway above. But this was how it looked around 1957 when the tranquility of the neat little station was momentarily disturbed as A3 Pacific No. 60051 *Blink Bonny,* **prior to rebuilding with a double chimney, hurried through on a northbound express.** *Peter Cookson.*

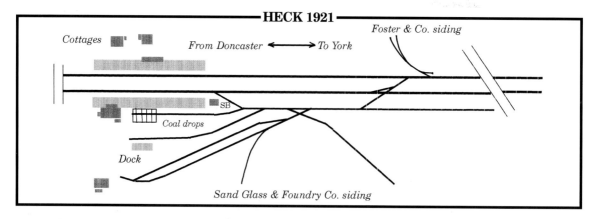

In summer, 1957, Heck was served by just two York-Doncaster passenger trains each way on Mondays to Saturdays. They left at 7.48 and 11.22am for Temple Hirst, Selby and York, and at 8.59am(9.1 Sats) and 5.29pm for Balne and Doncaster. There was no Sunday service. The station closed to passengers along with Riccall and Balne on 15th September, 1958.

The 1956 Handbook of Stations showed Heck as equipped to handle general goods, livestock, horse boxes and prize cattle vans. The private sidings were not reported. It closed to goods traffic on 29th April, 1963 but in 2002 a private siding serves the Plasmor building block company which has its own Fowler 0-4-0 diesel and despatches a train to Biggleswade and London each day.

Above: With the end of steam on the East Coast main line fast approaching, A3 No. 60044 *Melton* **heads the Up Anglo-Scottish Car Carrier near Heck at 4.14pm on 8th June, 1963.** *David Holmes.*

Two and a half miles south of Heck was Balne, the smallest station on the line. Along with its Up and Down platforms north of the level crossing it had, south of the crossing, just a trailing crossover, one siding with a loading dock and a headshunt on the Up side with cottages alongside. Opposite the main station buildings, on the Up side, were some stables and, across the road at the entrance to the goods yard, a weighbridge. Balne station closed to passengers on 15th September, 1958 and to goods on 6th July, 1964.

Three miles south of Balne was Moss, the last public station in the North Eastern Region. Slightly larger than Balne, it had a goods yard with two sidings on the Down side plus a trailing crossover, headshunt, loading dock and a yard crane, but the station closed to both passengers and goods on 8th June, 1953.

Below: Joan Croft Junction in the 1970s with a pair of Class 37 locos, 37018 leading, heading an Immingham to Leeds Hunslet East petroleum train onto the Down East Coast main line. The train has come down the spur from the West Riding & Grimsby line which connects the Grimsby-Doncaster line to the Doncaster-Leeds line via the overbridge in the distance. It will reach Leeds via the Selby Canal-West curve. There used to be a staff halt here even though the signal box was abolished in the 1930s when Shaftholme Junction took over control. *Peter Cookson.*

Above: The York & North Midland from York to Gascoigne Wood, Milford and Normanton was the Selby district's second main line and the first north-south line to be opened. Burton Salmon became a key junction where the line to Knottingley and Sheffield via Pontefract left the original route to Normanton. It was notable for having two signal boxes, one having replaced the other.

Here, B1 4-6-0 No. 61002 *Impala* passes the old signal box with a Manchester Victoria-York express while 9F 2-10-0 No. 92153 approaches the replacement box with a freight from York to the Midlands via the Pontefract line. Burton Salmon station closed in 1959 and there is no junction here now, just a divergence of the Normanton and Pontefract lines. *Peter Cookson*

THE YORK & NORTH MIDLAND

Below: Going north from Burton Salmon, the first station was Monk Fryston. In this 1950s scene, a young girl covers here ears as B1 No. 61295 roars under the NER-pattern footbridge with an express from Wakefield to York via Selby on 4th May, 1958. The Goods lines running from Milford to Burton Salmon are behind the Up platform on the left. *D. Butterfield / N.E.Stead collection.*

Above: The YNMR route was part of the East Coast main line until the York-Selby-Shaftholme route was opened in 1871. Every so often, it returned to its origins when ECML trains were diverted via Knottingley and Askern.

Class A2 Pacific No. 60539 *Bronzino* passes through Monk Fryston in the southbound direction with a diverted express for King's Cross on 4th May, 1958. Served mainly by York-Sheffield stopping trains, Monk Fryston station closed to passengers on 14th September, 1959. Goods facilities which could handle livestock, furniture vans and various machines on wheels as well as general freight, were reduced to a public delivery siding on the same date and withdrawn completely on 4th May, 1964, though a private siding remained at nearby Milford to serve John Smith's brewery maltings. Nothing remains of the station in 2002. *D. Butterfield / N.E.Stead collection*

Below: Just a short distance down the line towards York was Milford Junction station, built for passengers forced to change trains when Hudson withdrew the Leeds & Selby service and redirectedits passengers via his York-Leeds Hunslet Lane trains. The full Leeds-Selby service was restored in 1869 and Milford's role declined, the station closing in 1904. The redundant buildings hung on for another 60 years, finally being demolished in the 1960s.

Here, York's B16/2 4-6-0 No. 61455 passes the old station with an express for the Sheffield direction. *K. Hoole / N.E.Stead collection.*

Above: With the John Smith's maltings on its right, Black Five 4-6-0 No. 44688 draws up to the signal at Milford and waits to take the curve to Gascoigne Wood with the summer Saturday Liverpool Exchange to Scarborough express. Milford station and some of the sidings are visible beyond the end of the train, while more sidings can be seen on the right. *K. Hoole / N.E.Stead collection.*

Below: In a scene typical of the traditional railway, WD 2-8-0 No. 90578 forges a southbound class H freight past Sherburn-in-Elmet station on 22nd April, 1963. As it approaches Sherburn North signal box it is passing a malthouse for Tetley's brewery. With brewing centres in nearby Tadcaster, Leeds and York, the barley growing landscape hereabouts was dotted with maltings. *Peter Rose*

Above: The name recalling its Dark Ages origins when this part of the country was the ancient British kingdom of Elmet, this was Sherburn-in-Elmet station looking south on 16th October, 1966, the nameboard and other fittings still intact over a year since closure on 13th September, 1965.

Beyond the crossing gates is the Down Goods line from Sherburn South while the goods yard and loading dock are hidden by the signal box and waiting shelter. An occupation crossing crossed the Down Goods and other lines, and the 1960 Sectional Appendix stated that trains, if 49 wagons or more, must not be left fouling the crossing. If necessary guards had to split the train and make a gap in the wagons to clear the crossing for foot and vehicle traffic.

The station remained intact after closure and it was a simple matter to reopen it in July, 1984, since when it has been served mainly by the diminishing York-Sheffield service. Since reopening, the wooden shelter on the left has been replaced by a bus shelter. *P.B.Booth/N.E.Stead collection*

Below: A mile and a half further north, the YNM was joined by the direct Leeds-York line opened in 1869. The Leeds line curves in from the right following its 1 in 133-145 descent from Micklefield as 4F 0-6-0 No. 44467 of Leeds Stourton shed approaches from the south with an enthusiasts' special at 11.25am on 27th September, 1963. Church Fenton South signal box, abolished in 1970 when control was transferred to Church Fenton North, stands above the last coach. *David Holmes*

Above: Jubilee 4-6-0 No. 45698 *Mars* from Liverpool Bank Hall shed threads between the glazed canopies and wooden buildings of Church Fenton station on the Down Normanton line with the 10.5am Liverpool Exchange to York express at 1.25pm on Sunday 10th May, 1959.

The station was modernised in the late 1980s which, as well as renewal of the footbridge, inevitably meant demolition of all the wooden platform buildings and canopies, and their replacement with bus shelters. *David Holmes*

Below: The same location viewed from the footbridge ramp at 11.2am on 27th September, 1963 as O1 2-8-0 No. 63863 from Staveley Great Central shed heads a class H freight along the Up Normanton line. Although lacking its old charm, Church Fenton is a very busy junction nowadays with a fair amount of freight still to be observed on the Normanton lines. *David Holmes.*

Above: Wakefield B1 4-6-0 No. 61131 makes its way through platform 1 on the Up Normanton line with the 1.20pm York to Wakefield Westgate at 1.33pm on Sunday 8th May, 1960. Note the ornate platform light on the left. *David Holmes*

Below: The daily Newcastle to Manchester Red Bank empty newspaper vans were noted for their double heading combinations. They certainly excelled on 8th May, 1960 when A3 Pacific No. 60092 *Fairway* was being piloted by B1 No. 61021 *Reitbok* on the Leeds line through Church Fenton at 3.22pm. *David Holmes*
At this time, Church Fenton still had its full layout, semaphore signals and water columns, the line to Tadcaster and Wetherby curving away to the left beyond the buildings and the Wetherby bay still in situ on the extreme left. The semaphores were replaced by colour lights in November, 1968.

Above: V2 2-6-2 No. 60810 makes a spectacular start from the platform 3 road with a York-bound freight on 20th April, 1961, having been held for the Worcester-York express hauled by Jubilee No. 45579 to pass. The V2 has been routed via the Down Goods from Sherburn and is signalled to regain the Down Normanton. The water tank beyond the splitting signals on the far side was a signal box prior to 1904. *Peter Rose*

Below: Ulleskelf station was, and still is, a simple island platform situated between the Up and Down Normanton lines. Here, B16/2 4-6-0 No. 61457 hauls a class F unfitted goods along the Up Normanton at 3.8pm on 8th November, 1961. *David Holmes*

The station became unstaffed in 1972 when the platform buildings were stripped away. As can be seen, the goods yard on the right was well equipped with loading dock, goods shed and coal drops. though no permanent yard crane was provided. It closed in April, 1964. In 2002, the station is still open and served by a small number of York-Sheffield and Manchester Victoria trains.

Above: K1 2-6-0 No. 62029 makes a dramatic approach to Bolton Percy as it heads back to York with a returning pick-up goods at 4.4pm on 8th August, 1964. *David Holmes*

Below: Looking north from the overbridge at Bolton Percy affords a good view of the station area as Black Five 4-6-0 No. 44990 passes on the Down Normanton with vans for York at 5.37pm on 8th August, 1964. *David Holmes*

Like its neighbours at Church Fenton and Ulleskelf, Bolton Percy was built in the early 20th century when the Church Fenton-York section was quadrupled. Buildings from the original station, the last of which were demolished in 1997, are just visible on the left behind the telegraph pole. It is interesting to note how much thought for passengers was put into the design of the rebuilt station - ramps instead of steps and glazed screens at the ends of the platform canopies to protect passengers from the wind. Bolton Percy closed to goods in April, 1964 and to passengers on 13th September, 1965, there being practically nothing to see of the station in 2002.

Above: South Milford station looking towards Gascoigne Wood and Selby on 2nd July, 1967, still with the original low platform and station master's house on the right. The signal box, if open at the time of this picture, was soon to be closed though it remained standing in the 1980s by which time railings and a cycle rack had been added in front of the old shelter on the right. The small goods yard was just beyond the signal box but, having closed in 1963, all connections had been removed well before 1967. *P. B. Booth / N. E. Stead collection.*

The station became unstaffed in the late 1980s and by 2001 all buildings had gone though it thankfully remains open, served by hourly Selby-Leeds-Bradford-Manchester Victoria trains.

MILFORD-SELBY-STADDLETHORPE

Below: Gascoigne Wood was one of the biggest hump marshalling yards on the NER and needed some the biggest shunting engines to work its big hump on the north side. Working there on 31st January, 1959 was Selby's massive 3 cylinder T1 4-8-0T No. 69912. *Neville Stead*

Above: Among the big tank engines once allocated to Selby for shunting Gascoigne Wood yard was this beast, Great Central 1902-design Q1 0-8-0T No. 69933, seen in the yard during the mid-1950s. These engines where not as old as they seemed, being 1940s rebuilds of GC tender engines, but with only two cylinders they were no match for the T1s on the big hump. *Ernest Sanderson.*

Gascoigne Wood yard had two shunting humps - the big hump on the north side and the small hump on the south side.

The big hump was used for everything that arrived, and the small hump for departing wagons, mostly empties returning to collieries.

Above: The last public station at Gascoigne Wood closed in 1902, but in 1907 a timber platform was provided for marshalling yard staff and their families living nearby, and it remained in use until the yard closed on 2nd November, 1959. The platform is visible on the right as another Selby T1, No. 69921, performs hump shunting duties at 2.35pm on 3rd April, 1959. Wagons were pushed over the hump at 1.5 mph. Following transfer to Tyne Dock, 69921 became the last survivor of its class. *David Holmes.*

Above: While Gascoigne Wood's purpose was the transfer of coal traffic between West Riding pits and Hull and Goole, it took on a completely different role on the busy summer Saturdays of the 1950s and early 1960s. That was when the seaside passenger trains which took holidaymakers to and from the Yorkshire coast paused there to either take water or swap their London Midland engines for North Eastern engines. The NE engines, which took the trains to Bridlington, Filey Holiday Camp or Scarborough and back, usually via the Market Weighton line and to the delight of young spotters along the way, were provided by Selby shed. After that shed closed in 1959, the NE engines were sent from York each Saturday morning.

In this 1950s view, Liverpool Bank Hall Black Five 4-6-0 No. 44688 sets off with the returning 11.25am Scarborough-Liverpool Exchange, having taken over from a Selby loco. The staff halt is on the left. *K. Hoole/N.E.Stead collection.*

SUMMER SATURDAY TRAINS BOOKED TO CHANGE ENGINES AT GASCOIGNE WOOD PEAK SUMMER, 1955		

Arr	Dep	
10.15	10.23am	8.20am Chesterfield Midland-Scarborough Londesborough Rd.
11am	11.16am	9.35am Sowerby Bridge-Scarborough Londesborough Rd.
12.3	12.18pm	9.5am Liverpool Exchange-Scarborough Londesborough Rd.
12.45	1pm	10.57am Scarborough Londesborough Rd.-Derby
1.32	1.47pm	11.20am Scarborough Londesborough Rd.-Liverpool Exchange
2.34	2.43pm	12.25pm Scarborough Londesborough Rd.-Sowerby Bridge

Between 8.28am and 4.10pm on high summer Saturdays, 14 other passenger trains were booked to take water at Gascoigne Wood. They were the 7.12 and 8.36am Sheffield Victoria-Bridlington, the 8.55am Bradford Exchange-Bridlington, 8.5am Blackburn-Scarborough, 10.30am Sheffield Victoria-Filey Holiday Camp, 9.55am Manchester London Rd.-Scarborough Londesborough Rd., 9.50am Gloucester Eastgate-Filey Holiday Camp, 9.20am Filey Holiday Camp-King's Norton, 9.50am Filey Holiday Camp-Sheffield Victoria, 10am Scarborough Londesborough Rd.-Manchester London Rd., 11.55am Scarborough Londesborough Rd.-Leicester Central, 1.17pm Bridlington-Sheffield Victoria, 2.45pm Bridlington-Bradford Exchange, and the 1.50pm Scarborough-Blackburn.

The five and a quarter-mile Cawood, Wistow & Selby Light Railway was one of those delightfully rustic branch lines which until the 1960s one could suddenly discover running along the edge of many a field or minor road.

Although there were sidings along the way, its only intermediate station was at Wistow where, above, the train crew have just opened the crossing gates for J72 0-6-0T No.68686 to proceed with the branch goods in late April, 1960. Complete closure of the branch on 2nd May was barely a week away. The J72 still carries its Selby shedplate but was a York engine following the closure of Selby shed the previous September. *Hugh Davies*

Below: The simple but well-built station and goods facilities at Wistow are shown to good effect here. The 1956 Handbook of Stations shows Wistow as being able to handle coal, mineral and side to side traffic in wagon loads. *Neville Stead collection.*

Apart from the two stations, the Cawood branch also had intermediate sidings at South Lane (Cawood), Crosshills, Flaxley, Leeds Road(or Thorpe Road), Selby Common and Wistow Junction (Selby.) All except Leeds Road were public sidings able to handle coal, minerals and side to side traffic in wagon loads.

Above: The branch terminus at Cawood with BR 204hp(Class 03) diesel shunter D2063 and a brake van railtour in the old passenger platform on 27th April, 1960. Taken from the loading dock, the picture shows the station buildings and small goods shed. It was originally intended that the line would continue to Church Fenton. *David Lawrence.*

Below: Not only are the staff and the engine real classics, but so are the enthusiasts - true gricers! All are gathered for a farewell trip on the Cawood branch with J72 No. 68686 in April, 1960. *Hugh Davies.*

Cawood station was equipped to handle parcels and miscellaneous traffic, livestock, horse boxes and prize cattle vans, and carriages and motor cars by parcels train as well as general goods.

In 1960, the Cawood class K goods trip was booked to leave Selby at 11am(Monday-Friday), call Wistow when required and arrive Cawood at 11.35. The return was booked to depart Cawood at 11.55, call Wistow when required and arrive back in Selby at 12.30pm.

SELBY WEST SIGNAL BOX - London Road level crossing. Terminating trains for the New Yard from the east must run clear of the crossing up to the Up Main starting signal so as to allow the crossing gates to be opened when necessary for road traffic to pass before the train is set back into the yard. The gates will be opened as soon as the van of the train has reached signal No. 20 - Shunting Up main. Drivers must not move back until the Backing Signal is lowered and must keep a careful look-out for any signals given them by the guard or signalman. *BR Eastern Region(North) Sectional Appendix, 1969.*

Above: Viewed from Selby West signal box, Hull Dairycoates K3 2-6-0 No. 61945 comes off the loop from Selby South with a class F goods on 24th May, 1961. Originally called Brayton Gates, then Cawood Junction, this box has controlled all Selby's railway since 1973, a job which once required seven boxes. In 2002 it bore two different nameboards - Selby West and Selby. The coaling plant of the closed Selby motive power depot stands proud in the distance. *Peter Rose.*

Below: On 23rd March, 1959, Ivatt Class 4 2-6-0 No. 43057 hauls a lengthy Through Freight past its new home depot on the goods line from Selby West to the station, a line abandoned in 1969. On the left, the old coaling stage still stands alongside the 1930s mechanical coaling tower. This whole area has since been obliterated. Walk down Portholme Road now and you would never believe it bordered a major railway complex. *Neville Stead.*

Above: A trio of J39 0-6-0s, standard Selby trip freight power, stand around the turntable in one of the two roundhouses on 22nd August,1959. *P.B.Booth / N.E.Stead collection.*

Although a 'C' shed, coded 50C in the BR North Eastern Region's York District, Selby was a big shed with a substantial allocation of engines of mouthwatering variety. Its main purpose was to provide engines and crews for the many mineral trips connecting the collieries around Castleford and Pontefract to the yard at Gascoigne Wood, plus tank engines for shunting at Gascoigne Wood and other local yards. It also supplied engines for local passenger and goods traffic along the branches to Market Weighton, Goole and Cawood.

Its allocation included the big North Eastern T1 class 4-8-0 hump shunting tanks as well as Great Central style 0-8-0 tanks and a range of smaller tank engines for lighter shunting, including the small hump at Gascoigne Wood. Main line goods engines included various 0-6-0s and 0-8-0s while the D20 4-4-0s were its best known passenger engines, some later replaced by the slightly more modern D49s. The Sentinel steam railcar *Hope* was allocated there in the 1940s for work on the Goole branch until replaced by the older but more conventional ex-NER G5 0-4-4Ts. A converted Leyland bus was based there in the 1920s for working the Cawood branch service until it was destroyed when its lean-to shed alongside the coal stage burnt down. Selby depot consisted of two adjacent roundhouses, each with one turntable. The old shed, completed in 1871, had two access roads and 18 stalls from the turntable while the new shed, completed in 1898, had two access roads and 22 stalls.

The impending closure of Gascoigne Wood marshalling yard and dieselisation of local passenger services rendered Selby MPD redundant and it closed in September, 1959, its remaining work switched to York. The 50C shedcode was given to the diesel depot at Hull Botanic Gardens. After some years of dereliction, the Selby shed site and that of the Selby West-Selby station goods lines were redeveloped and in 2002 were largely occupied by new housing, a police station and council offices.

Locomotives allocated to Selby, August, 1950

D20 4-4-0: 62340/1/8/61/3/6/74/6/8/81/2/6/95; **Q5 0-8-0:** 63280/5/63319/36; **Q6 0-8-0:** 63348/78/82/7/95/ 63406/ 8/29/31/6/40/8/9/51/6; **J21 0-6-0:** 65039/42/65105; **J27 0-6-0:** 65793/65827/44/8/9/ 51/6; **G5 0-4-4T:** 67250/86; **Y1 and Y3 4w Sentinel:** 68143/56/8/61; **J71 0-6-0T:** 68268; **J73 0-6-0T:** 68356/7/62; **J77 0-6-0T:** 68399/68433; **A8 4-6-2T:** 69867/79; **Q1 0-8-0T:** 69931/3. Total: 60

Above: A cross section of power around one of the turntables in Selby shed on 5th May, 1957. Q6 0-8-0 No. 63450 is joined by D49/2 4-4-0s 62772 *The Sinnington* and 62755 *The Bilsdale*. *P.B.Booth/N.E.Stead collection.*

Left: One of Selby's smaller goods tender engines, J25 0-6-0, LNER No. 2073 in the shed yard.
G.W.Sharpe collection.

Locomotives allocated to Selby, June, 1955

Ivatt Class 4 2-6-0: 43052/96/7/8/123; **B16 4-6-0:** 61474; **D20 4-4-0:** 62343/78/81/86/95; **D49 4-4-0:** 62736 *The Bramham Moor/* 62740 *The Bedale/* 62761*The Derwent;* **Q6 0-8-0:** 63378/82/95/ 63406/23/5/9/40/8/9/ 50/1; **J39 0-6-0:** 64725/30/64850/64904/22; **J25 0-6-0:** 65683/98; **J27 0-6-0:** 65861/75/81/5/8/91; **G5 0-4-4T:** 67250/86; **Y1 & Y3 4w Sentinel:** 68150/8/80; **J73 0-6-0T:** 68356/7/62; **J77 0-6-0T:** 68406/29; **A8 4-6-2T:** 69877; **Q1 0-8-0T:** 69931/3; **BR 4MT 2-6-0:** 76021; **WD 2-8-0:** 90670. Total: 54

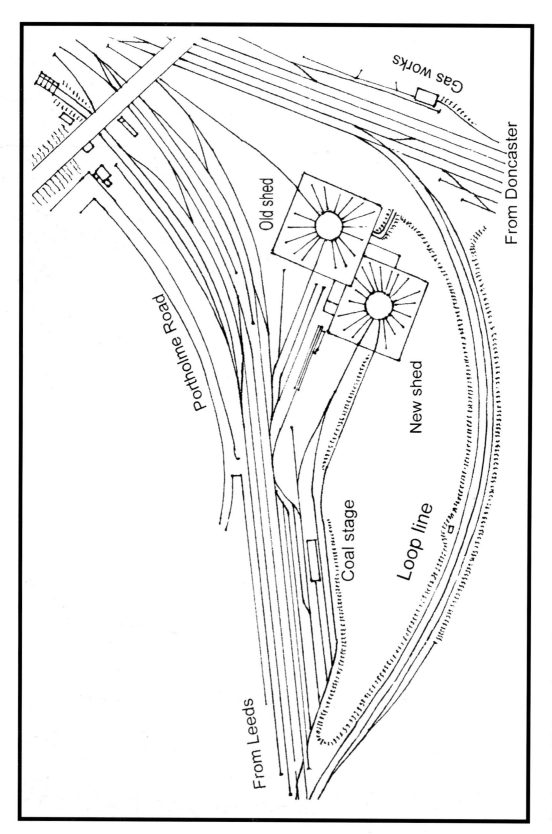

The layout of Selby engine shed as it was around 1920. *Not to scale.* The mechanical coaling plant has yet to be built alongside the existing coaling stage, and so has the curve connecting the Loop line to the Doncaster line at Canal Junction.

Above: The variety of Selby's own locos was further enriched by the visitors that came on shed. Here, B16/1 4-6-0 No. 61469, K3 2-6-0 No. 61895 and a 9F too dirty to identify, stand outside the old shed in the late 1950s. The south end of Selby station can be seen just beyond the overbridge. *G. W. Sharpe collection.*

Below: Standing outside the new shed at 2.29pm on 29th September, 1956 were J27 0-6-0 No. 65888 and J39 0-6-0 No. 64904. The new shed was on the south side of the old shed. A Gresley coach stands behind the muck heap. *David Holmes.*

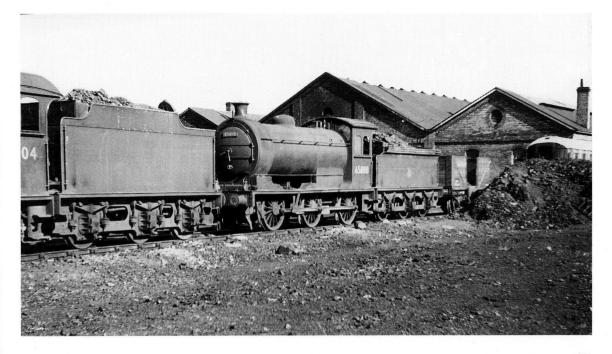

Two of Selby's little North Eastern tank engines.
Above: Class J73 0-6-0T No. 68357 wearing pilot headlamps outside the old shed at 2.40pm on 29th September, 1956. Designed by Wilson Worsdell, these engines were introduced in 1891.
David Holmes.

Below: Inside the shed, J71 0-6-0T No. 68230. Designed by T.W. Worsdell, this class was introduced in 1886. *G. W. Sharpe collection.*

Subject to certain conditions, locomotives could assist passenger trains at the rear when diverted via Selby West-Canal, Selby Canal-Selby South and Selby South-Selby West because of a blockage on their normal route. But when the train was being drawn by the pilot, the train engine at the rear was not permitted to provide any assistance.

Summer, 1960: D49s brought out of store in Hull have a top link Monday-Friday duty through Goole, working the 8.26pm Doncaster-Hull which is the Hull portion of the Yorkshire Pullman. They also work the 8.47am and 5.53pm Hull-Doncaster and 1.44pm return. On Saturdays they work the 11.16am Scarborough-Liverpool as far as Goole.

16.7.60: Type 4 D283 pilots A1 60128 *Bongrace* on the 9.40am York to King's Cross as far as Doncaster from where it returns with the 8.40am King's Cross-Edinburgh. Double heading of Pacifics and Type 4 diesels for this purpose was normal at this time.

Above: The elegant D20 4-4-0s introduced in 1899 were probably the best loved of all Selby's engines. D20/1 No. 62378, as rebuilt with superheated boiler, stands at Selby South on 30th August, 1954. Compare this loco with 1234 in original condition on page 39.

Selby was a stronghold of the D20s during their later years, using them for local main line passenger trains and other light work during the winter, and for assisting heavy holiday trains to the coast via Market Weighton in the summer. On 8th May, 1952 No. 62378, hauling the 160-ton 11am Doncaster-York semi-fast from Selby, reached 59mph by the time it passed Riccall and passed Escrick(6.7 miles) in just over eight minutes. *Brian Morrison*

Below: A rather different type of engine based at Selby for push-pull or railmotor trains on the Goole branch were the G5 0-4-4Ts introduced by the NER in 1894. No. 67286 waits in the bay platform at Selby station with the 3.24pm to Goole on 29th September, 1956. In 2002, trains to Manchester Victoria via Bradford and the Calder Valley use this platform. *David Holmes.*

Two classic views of the Goole railmotor worked by Selby stalwart G5 No. 67250.
Above: Awaiting departure from the main northbound platform in May, 1952.
B.G.Tweed / N.E.Stead collection.

Below: At Selby South in early British Railways days, c.1949. The second coach appears to be an ex-Great Central 12-wheel railmotor vehicle. The slotted signals on the gantry have already given way to the new upper quadrant type. *J.W. Hague / N.E.Stead collection.*

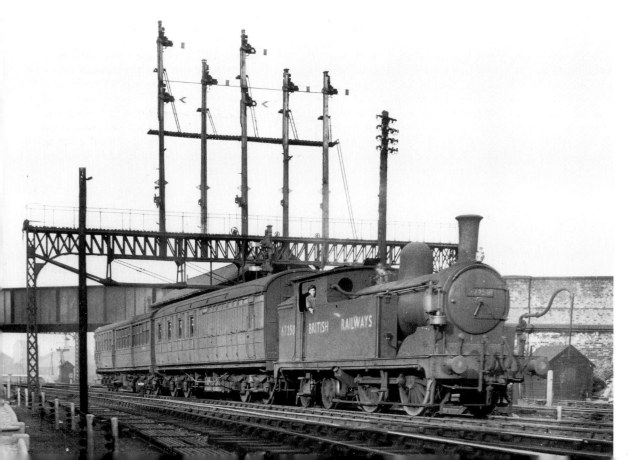

Above: In 1957 the G5s gave way to diesel multiple units on the Goole branch. Here, viewed from the East Coast main line, one of the new fangled culprits, a three-car set built by the Birmingham Railway Carriage & Wagon Co.(later Class 104) leaves Brayton Junction with a service to Goole.
Peter Cookson

Having a passing loop, Barlow was the only two-platform station on the Selby-Goole branch and it had the only intermediate signal box between Brayton and Oakhill Junction, though the passenger station was of the same timber construction as the others.

Following closure of the Goole line as a through route in 1964, the Brayton-Barlow section was retained to serve the railway tip until that closed in 1984, and since then the track has been used for training track maintenance machine operators. The 2 miles 511 yards stump from Brayton Junction was worked under One Engine in Steam regulations. The maximum line speed in both directions was 30mph. The only additional running line remaining was the passing loop at Barlow accommodating 42 wagons, engine and brake van. A ground frame released by Annett's key was provided to control entrance to the tip sidings. The key was kept in Brayton box to be collected by guards before entering the branch and returned on leaving. The Ministry of Defence depot at Barlow still boasted a 60cm gauge railway system in the 1970s with two diesel locomotives, No.27 was a Ruston & Hornsby built in 1944 and No. 32, a Hunslet built in 1937.

Left: With the all-timber construction used for many smaller stations in the early 1900s, this was Drax Hales station, renamed Drax in 1961.
Peter Cookson

Above: The Selby-Goole branch passed over the Hull & Barnsley Railway at Drax. Here, a two-car DMU crosses the intersection bridge in the 1950s. This whole area is now occupied by the giant Drax power station, part of the Goole line embankment being used as a landscaping screen. *Roger Bastin.*

Below: Dr. Beeching had condemned the Goole branch by the time this 1960s photo was taken of a Hull Botanic Gardens Cravens two-car DMU entering Drax with a service to Selby. The two passengers include a heavily-laden angler with Beatle haircut. Note the trim gardens across the track from the platform. *Peter Cookson.*

SHORT MEMORIES

19-21.7.60: The first Trans-Pennine DMU makes trial runs between Leeds and Hull. Departing Leeds 3.30pm it was scheduled to reach Hull in 59 mins., returning to Leeds in 63 mins.

20.7.60: Caprotti valve gear Black Five 4-6-0 44753 works the 9am Hull-Liverpool Lime St.

23.8.60: A1 Pacific 60153 *Flamboyant* heads the 9am Hull-Liverpool.

Easter Sunday, 1961: A4 No. 60002 *Sir Murrough Wilson* is on a returning Newcastle-Hull excursion and the next day's 8pm Hull to York class C freight.

Above: Back in the 1950s, Selby's Ivatt Class 4 2-6-0 No. 43123 rolls into Drax with what was probably the 5.8pm Selby to Goole, a conventional loco-hauled train rather than push-pull. *Roger Bastin.*

Below: The first stop out of Goole for this Selby-bound Birmingham RC&W 4-car DMU was Airmyn, pictured in June, 1964 with nil passengers and the Beeching axe about to descend. The station was previously called Airmyn & Rawcliffe but was renamed by BR in 1961. *D.P.Leckonby*

Left: Pictures of goods trains on the Selby-Goole line are not so common. In this shot, a 2-6-4T from Goole shed is heading west with with what may well be the 6.15pm Goole to Selby freight. The engine is, however, carrying class H headlamps but the 6.15, the line's only booked through goods train, was class D. *Norman Ling / Peter Rose colln.*

Besides its three stations and the establishments at Barlow, the Selby-Goole line had a coal siding at Brayton, and sidings near Airmyn at Firth Drain and Newland public delivery siding.

Drax goods yard was equipped with a 2 ton crane and could handle all kinds of freight. Barlow could handle furniture vans, carriages, motor cars, portable engines and machines on wheels plus carriages and cars by passenger or parcels train; Airmyn could handle livestock, horse boxes and prize cattle vans and carriages and cars by passenger or parcels train.

Right: One can only ponder at this 1950s picture of a very lengthy football special hauled by one of Selby's Ivatt 2-6-0s.

If it is carrying supporters for a match between Selby Town and Goole Town, as suggested by local motive power, then it is a measure of the support which even teams in the lower leagues could command in the 1950s, especially if a derby game or a cup tie. *Norman Ling / P. Rose colln.*

Above: Back at Selby. York B16/2 4-6-0 No. 61421 has an apparently clear road ahead as it comes through the station with a train of vans on 19th June, 1963. The scene is deceptive though, as 61421 later reversed its class K trip freight, probably from BOCM, into the yard on the right where Ivatt Class 2 2-6-0 No. 46413 awaited departure with a Goole branch pick-up. *Peter Rose.*

Below: WD 2-8-0 No.90482 plods through the station with the 12.45pm Hull Outward Yard to Leeds special class H on 6th March, 1963. *Peter Rose.*

Remnants of Selby's first railway in the 1970s.
Above: The business end of the Leeds & Selby terminus looking north towards the end of the line and station buildings. On the right are sheds which were still in use as a railway freight depot by the Viking Shipping Co. The back wall of the present day station is on the left.

Below: A truly remarkable survivor - remains of the wooden jetty where 1830s passengers, having arrived by train from Leeds, boarded the steamboat for the rest of their journey to Hull. The jetties were built on wooden piles driven 25ft into the river bed and this portion still stands 168 years later in 2002. *Both photos by the late Sydney Martin.*

SHORT MEMORIES

April, 1961: After a spell hauled by Brush Type 2 diesels, the 4.35pm Hull-Liverpool Central reverts to steam haulage by Sheffield Darnall B1s.

26 & 27.4.61: The 5am Leeds-Hull and 1.50pm Hull-Leeds parcels, usually a Farnley Class 5 4-6-0, is hauled by A3 No. 60092 *Fairway.*

9.9.62: Winter timetable sees Hull-Doncaster local services dieselised or withdrawn and Hull-Goole services severely curtailed.

August, 1963: WDs 90072/81/132/273/406/51 transferred to Goole where 90186/228/ 461/75/ 531 are withdrawn.

Summer,1964: Rebuilding of Selby main station buildings includes modernisation of entrance hall, booking and parcels offices, buffet, waiting room and toilets besides replacement of gas lights with flourescent lights.

Summer,1964: Trans-Pennine DMU cars frequently have to be replaced by conventional Metro-Cammell vehicles.

Below: Despite being issued on 12th February, 1972, this ticket still shows 3rd class.

Above: One of just three trains to run all year round on weekdays from Selby to Market Weighton and Bridlington after the withdrawal of local services in 1954, the 9.28am from Leeds City is set in motion out of Selby and onto the swing bridge by B16/1 4-6-0 No. 61411 at 10.13am on 22nd July, 1960. Just two regular service trains ran in the other direction but on summer Saturdays the Market Weighton line had to accommodate nearly 40 extra trains. The tall masts carry various cables over the river at a height well clear of shipping. *Robert Anderson.*

Below: The sort of fascinating view which could once be enjoyed from a train on the swing bridge. Thought to be in the 1930s or 1940s, a steam dredger works on the river in front of Selby's famous toll bridge, while a jetty in Ousegate supports a steam-powered rail-mounted crane or grab used for unloading boats. *Ernest Sanderson / Stephen Chapman collection.*

Above: B1 4-6-0 No. 61218 on the very gentle fall to Selby swing bridge with a Hull to Leeds express on 23rd May, 1959. *Brian Morrison*

Below: The view from an East Coast express as it is hauled Yorkwards from the bridge by A4 Pacific No. 60013 *Dominion of New Zealand* on 30th July, 1962. Barlby signal box and level crossing are up ahead in the murk, the Up Hull and Goods lines are on the right and, among the trees, the BOCM sidings still used for internal rail movements in 2002. Spring points were used where the Up Hull line joined the Up Main to avoid carrying point rodding across the swing bridge from Selby North signal box. Barlby box survives in 2002 as a gate box for the crossing. *Peter Rose*

Above: Barlby North on 22nd June, 1963 with B1 4-6-0 No.61353 from Leeds Neville Hill shed passing the signal box as it approaches Selby with empty coaching stock off the Market Weighton line. The signal box had two frames, the signalmen working back to back. *Peter Rose*

BETWEEN BARLBY NORTH AND SELBY SOUTH SIGNAL BOXES -Working of Freight Trains.

Drivers of trains which are to travel on the Up main or Up Hull line from Barlby North and have been accepted by the signalman at Selby South under the Warning Arrangement will receive a Warning at Barlby North which will be an indication that the line is clear to Selby South Home signals only, no warning being given at the intermediate boxes, e.g. Barlby and Selby North, except as follows: In case of trains accepted by Barlby from Barlby North at Line Clear and brought to a stand at Barlby Home signals, or trains on the Goods lines. Drivers, when Barlby Home signal is lowered, must take this as an indication that the line is clear to Selby South Home signals only and must regulate the speed of trains accordingly. *BR Eastern Region(Northern Area) Sectional Appendix, 1969.*

Below: Looking east at Barlby North on 22nd June, 1963 with the Market Weighton line diverging to the left, the Hull line straight on and the connections to Selby sugar factory on the right. All except the Market Weighton line(closed 1965) remains in use in 2002, the closed sugar factory now used as a rail freight terminal by Selby Storage. The Market Weighton line could be worked as a single track as far as Cliffe Common using Staff and Ticket over the Down line, provision being made for this at Barlby North box during the second world war when the Up line was used for wagon storage. *Peter Rose.*

Just three miles out of Selby on the Market Weighton line was Cliffe Common, a particularly interesting junction for this was where the Derwent Valley Light Railway came in from York. The DVLR was noteworthy because it remained privately owned, even escaping nationalization, to the very end. Although the Cliffe Common-Wheldrake section closed in 1964, the last stretch between Dunnington and York remained in business until September, 1981.

In both its early and final years, the DVLR had its own engines but for much of its time it hired engines from the LNER and then BR. Here, York shed's J25 0-6-0 No. 65714 awaits its return to York from the DVLR bay platform at Cliffe Common station on 14th August, 1959.

D. Butterfield / N.E.Stead collection

Left: A 1950s view showing the DVLR platform at Cliffe Common on the right and the NER Market Weighton line platforms on the left. The DVLR platform had not seen regular passenger trains since the DVLR's short-lived service was withdrawn in the 1920s, while the main line platforms were closed in 1954.

The old Manchester Sheffield & Lincolnshire Railway 6-wheel passenger brake was moved to Elvington when the Cliffe Common end closed in 1964.

Neville Stead collection

Above: In the mid-1950s, J21 0-6-0 No. 65064 was brought from Darlington to work a railtour along the DVLR. Here the special waits among stacks of timber for its departure back to York. During the 1950s it was common practice for timber arriving by ship at Hull Docks to be brought out to East Riding stations for storage until required, any spare goods yard space being utilised, and this seems to be the obvious reason for the stacks here.
Photo by the late Rev. John Parker.

Below: A rustic view from the platform. Another train, this time the normal goods hauled by a J25, awaits its return to York, the DVLR's regular brake van(of South Eastern & Chatham Railway origin) behind the loco. *David Lawrence*

Above: Hemingbrough, three miles east of Selby, in the 1950s with B1 4-6-0 No. 61237 *Geoffrey H. Kitson* on a long stopping train for Hull. The station closed to passengers in November, 1967 but the signalbox was in use until late 1997. *H. B. Priestley / N. Stead colln.*

Centre and bottom: Howden station and its beautifully kept buildings, or North Howden as it was known until the early 1960s. Although these views were taken as recently as 1997, much has changed. Resignalling bringing the line under the control of Selby box has seen the semaphore signals replaced by colour lights and the box closed though it still stood complete with nameboard in March, 2001.

Above: It is the first week of June, 1967, York shed is supposed to have closed to steam on the 6th and the end of steam is imminent everywhere else in this part of Yorkshire. Yet this was the dramatic scene at Staddlethorpe - Leeds Holbeck-based Jubilee 4-6-0 No. 45697 *Achilles*, working off York shed, tearing through the station with the 11.45 Hull to York via Selby. At this time, steam was used on the 08.18 York-Selby-Hull and 11.45 return for the purpose of passing out firemen who would surely not be needed for much longer. By this time, the 17.08 York-Selby-Hull was being worked by York's brand new English Electric Type 1(Class 20) diesels. *Ernest sanderson*

Below: On the approach to Staddlethorpe station, the driver of B1 No. 61158 has to brake hard for the Goole turnoff with his Hull-Sheffield Victoria express on 29th June, 1964. On the right, beyond the cabin, wagons are prepared for removal by the pick-up, including a creosote tank from Messrs Gabriel, Wade & English, suppliers of telegraph poles. *Peter Rose*

Above: The afore-mentioned pick-up has duly arrived in charge of Hull Dairycoates stalwart B1 No. 61256, collected the wagons and received the road to continue on its way. Peter Rose's Triumph Herald graces the platform. In 1974 Staddlethorpe was renamed Gilberdyke and in 2002, despite much rationalisation, retains some semaphore signals and remains a good spot to photograph the line's few remaining freight trains.

Below: A clear view of Staddlethorpe Junction, also on 29th June, 1964, with the lines to Goole on the left and to Selby straight on. Because of the kink where the Up Selby crosses the Down Goole, only the Down line from Selby actually constitutes the longest stretch of straight track in Britain. Points of interest include the signalman's Lambretta scooter, and the private siding emerging through a gate on the right past a low shunt signal, marked on an old map as "from flax mill." In 2002, all additional lines have gone and only the double line junction remains, together with the turnout from an Up siding behind the station. Housing occupies the private siding area. *Both Peter Rose*

The 1969 BR Sectional Appendix shows the Gascoigne Wood-Staddlethorpe line as signalled by Absolute Block with signal boxes at Gascoigne Wood, Thorpe Gates, Selby West, Selby South, Selby North, Barlby, Barlby North, Hemingbrough, Wressle, Howden, Eastrington and Staddlethorpe. Maximum line speed was 70mph on main lines.

There were Up and Down Goods lines between Selby West and South, Up and Down platform lines at Selby station, Down Slow line from Selby North to Barlby North, two Up Goods lines from Barlby North to Barlby, an Up refuge siding for 67 wagons, engine and brake at Hemingbrough, and Up and Down refuge sidings for 54 and 61 wagons, engine and brake respectively at Howden. The Hemingbrough and Howden refuge sidings were abandoned in 1968.

Above: One of the handsome D20 4-4-0s, D20/2 No. 62386, restarts its local passenger train to Selby away from Staddlethorpe in the early 1950s. This engine had been rebuilt in the 1930s with long travel valves and a J39-style tender. *G.W. Sharpe collection.*

STADDLETHORPE-GOOLE

Below: A slightly more recent view.
Saltmarshe station and its unusually shaped signal box looking towards Gilberdyke in summer, 2001. The corner window affords the signalman a view down the road which crosses the line on a skew. Although served by only a handful of trains each day, Saltmarshe, which serves the pretty village of Laxton, seems well patronised and in the mid-1980s was said to be generating 12,000 passenger journeys a year.

Above: Goole swing bridge over the River Ouse, otherwise known as Skelton Bridge, on 21st August, 1966. It consists of five 116ft fixed spans and a 250ft swinging portion. The River Ouse here is wide with treacherous currents and many a master has lost control of his vessel and collided with the bridge. In 1973, a collison knocked one of the fixed spans on the left into the river. *Peter Rose.*

The mechanism operating Goole swing bridge used to be steam powered and the 1969 Eastern Region Sectional Appendix set out the following instructions for tipping the coal supply:

Coal for use at the bridge is tipped through the bridge into lockers on the bridge jetty from the Up line. When it is necessary for coal to be tipped, the following method must be adopted:

Signal U4B must be maintained at Danger for the brake van to be detached, after which signal U4B should be released for the locomotive and wagons of coal to be drawn forward clear of the swinging portion of the bridge and Track Circuit No.7. No.1 point switch must then be operated, which will cause the points to be automatically set for the sand drag after the expiration of two minutes.

After the points have been set for the sand drag the locomotive and coal wagons must be hand signalled back to the required position. The wagons must then be properly secured by brakes and sprags and the locomotive again run forward clear of the swinging portion. Owing to Track circuit No.7 being occupied by the coal wagons, the emergency release must be operated to permit the bridge to be swung in order to tip the coal.

When the bridge is brought back into alignment for rail traffic the emergency release must be restored to the normal position, after which the locomotive must be hand signalled back to the wagons on the centre of the bridge. After attaching, the engine and wagons must run forward to clear Track Circuit No.7 to enable No.1 sand drag points to be set for the bridge. After reverse indication has been obtained, the locomotive and wagons must be hand signalled back to the remainder of the train standing at U4B signal. After the brake van has been attached, the trainmen must be instructed to pass the signal in the Danger position provided the line is clear. These instructions were deleted from the Appendix in February, 1975.

GOOLE NE GOODS YARD - Boothferry Road box. Trains for the NE goods yard must not exceed 10 vehicles. *Eastern Region(Northern Area) Sectional Appendix, 1969.*

SHORT MEMORIES

Summer,1964: The Halewood-Hull Ford car train is regularly steam, usually a Black Five or Jubilee 4-6-0, so is the 6.50pm Hull-Glasgow "Humber-Clyde" express goods, usually a York V2.

July, 1965: The transport minister approves closure of Bolton Percy and Sherburn stations but refuses the closure of Ulleskelf.

28.10.64: The Down Heart of Midlothian collides with derailed empty oil tanks from the 03.17 Millerhill-Ollerton freight at Henwick Hall. Deltic D9007 hauling the express sustains serious front end damage, four coaches are derailed but only two passengers are injured.

Above: After the closure of Goole engine shed, a former Lancashire & Yorkshire Railway establishment, the old North Eastern goods shed was converted into a fuelling and inspection point for diesel shunters ultimately outbased from Hull Botanic Gardens(50C) for working the docks. As rail traffic declined with only the odd shunter or two required, this small depot was also closed. It still remained in situ, disused with the fuel tank mounted on the loading dock, when photographed on 13th February, 1993 but the goods shed has since been demolished. The sidings and dock remain available for engineers' traffic along with a siding for turning back trains arriving from Leeds and Doncaster. The platform canopies of Goole station can be seen beyond the railbus. The space between the railbus and the siding is where the Up timber platform extension for London trains stood, the platform lights still in position! *Stephen Chapman.*

Above: The exterior of Goole NER goods shed, also on 13th February, 1993.
Stephen Chapman

On 6th November, 1971, Class 03 diesel shunters 2049(50D), 2100(50C) and 2157 (50D) were stabled at the goods shed.

Goole NER Goods depot could handle the full range of freight traffic, according to the 1956 Handbook of Stations. It had a 5-ton yard crane but loads of 50 tons could be handled by arrangement which would be by using a 50-ton hydraulic crane at Railway Dock.

Above: Goole no longer has direct trains to and from London. This is how they often looked in steam days with V3 2-6-2T No. 67635 of Hull Dairycoates shed at the head of the 10.20am King's Cross to Hull on 13th April, 1961. *Peter Cookson / N.E.Stead collection*

Below: Goole station looking from Boothferry Road level crossing towards a busy Hull-bound platform on 14th September, 1963 with one of Goole's Hunslet(Class 05) diesel shunters, No.D2611, performing a shunting move which has taken it into the station. *John Edgington.*

In 1968 the Staddlethorpe-Thorne line was signalled mostly by Absolute Block with intermediate signal boxes at Saltmarshe, Goole Bridge, Boothferry Road, Potter's Grange, Dutch River, Thorne Colliery and Thorne Moor. Track Circuit Block was in use between Saltmarshe and Boothferry Road while intermediate block signals were provided between Staddlethorpe and Saltmarshe. Up Goods lines, one Permissive Block and one with no block, were provided between Boothferry Road and Dutch River, and a Down Goods with Permissive Block between Dutch River and Potter's Grange. There were four Down refuge sidings between Potter's Grange and Boothferry Road. Maximum speed on main lines was 70mph with a 60mph restriction on the swing bridge.

Above: In this wonderfully atmospheric scene from 21st April, 1956, ex-L&Y 0-6-0 No. 52154 has just returned with the Saltmarshe trip, run round the train and is now preparing to propel it into the sidings. Notice the barrows, weighing machine and posters, all typical of the time. In 2002 the platform canopies are still there but the covered footbridge has been removed, passengers now using the Boothferry Road level crossing subway to cross the line. According to the indicator board, the next passenger train will be to Leeds City. *P.B.Booth / N.E.Stead collection*

SHORT MEMORIES

25.8.65: Type 4 D37 on the 08.15 Newcastle-Bristol fails at Bolton Percy. An unidentified tank engine sent from York hauls the train to Milford where D170 takes over.

1.1.66: BR Class 3 2-6-0s 77001 and 77012 transferred to Goole. 77001 is withdrawn by the end of the month.

3-5.2.66: The 08.52 Hull to King's Cross reverts to steam between Hull and Doncaster, hauled by B1 No. 61250 *A. Harold Bibby.*

Above: In the1960s, the entrance to Goole station was modernised and this was the result. Since this view was captured in August, 1998, even the 'new' entrance plus all the larger original buildings have been demolished and replaced by a large glass waiting room with integral ticket office that seems to be closed much of the time.

Above: Looking south from Goole station as a Cravens two-car DMU approaches with a service from Selby which has just come off the NER line from Oakhill Junction. This line, immediately behind the train, is gone now, the crossing gates have been replaced by lifting barriers and Boothferry Road box, now known simply as Goole, is now the only signal box in Goole. *Neville Stead*

Below: The 12.20pm Hull to King's Cross storms away from Goole station with K3 2-6-0 No. 61922 in command on 30th August, 1961. The lines on the far left are those to Oakhill Junction and Selby while the Up Goods lines are on the right. *Peter Rose.*

Above: One of the two daily Liverpool Central to Hull refreshment car expresses rolls past Potter's Grange and towards Goole behind Sheffield Darnall B1 No. 61112 on 13th April, 1961. Potter's Grange signal box is by the end of the train. *Peter Cookson/N.E.Stead collection*

SHORT MEMORIES

March, 1966: Five football specials from Southport to Hull for the FA Cup 5th round travel via Wakefield and Goole. Three are hauled by Black Five 4-6-0s and one by Britannia Pacific No. 70014 *Iron Duke*.

March, 1966: The 08.52 Hull-King's Cross is still steam as far as Doncaster.

18.4.66: New timetable sees the 08.52 retimed to 08.55 and routed via Selby.

Nov., 1966: About 75% of Goole-Wakefield freight is still steam, mostly 8F and WD 2-8-0s, 9F 2-10-0s, B1 and Class 5 4-6-0s.

Below: A never-to-be forgotten 1960s event was that Arctic 1962/63 winter. Here, in the thick of it, the 12.45pm Hull-King's Cross headed by B16/3 4-6-0 No. 61463 approaches Dutch River signal box on 25th January, 1963. That winter saw the B16s in demand for passenger services around Hull and York as diesel fuel turned to wax in the extreme cold. *Peter Rose*

THE LANKY & GOOLE DOCKS

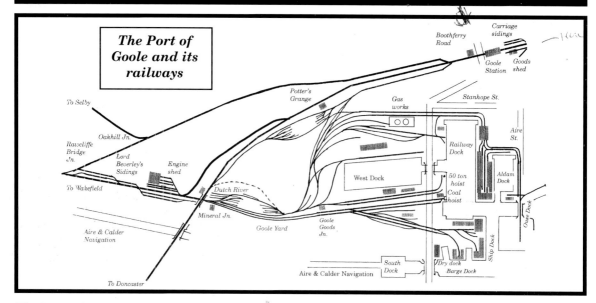

The Port of Goole and its railways

To Selby · Oakhill Jn. · Rawcliffe Bridge Jn. · Lord Beverley's Sidings · Engine shed · To Wakefield · Dutch River · Mineral Jn. · Aire & Calder Navigation · To Doncaster · Goole Yard · Potter's Grange · Gas works · West Dock · Goole Goods Jn. · Aire & Calder Navigation · South Dock · Stanhope St. · Railway Dock · 50 ton hoist · Coal hoist · Dry dock · Barge Dock · Boothferry Road · Carriage sidings · Goole Station · Goods shed · Aire St. · Aldam Dock · Ouse Dock · Ship Dock

The Lancashire & Yorkshire was the first railway to enter Goole and it was its railways that in the main served the docks, its origins remaining visible until the 1990s.

Below: At 2.6pm on 8th October, 1960 with Stanhope Street on the left, Lanky "Pug" 0-4-0ST No. 51244 on pilot 29 duty shunts containers and vans along the dock lines that were once the route to the L&Y's passenger station in Aire Street. The former L&Y goods offices on the left, built 1892, had been standing empty for more than 15 years by 2001. *David Holmes.*

Right: The view from Bridge Street level crossing on 12th October, 1988 with Stanhope Dock on the right and steel traffic in evidence. The railway has since been cut back to terminate on the south side of the crossing and a big warehouse fills this view.
Stephen Chapman

Below: On the same duty as opposite, fellow "Pug" No. 51222 stands at Bridge Street level crossing and the footbridge from which 51244 was photographed.
G.W.Sharpe collection

BRIDGE STREET LEVEL CROSSING: Drivers requiring to work trains over this crossing must not foul the crossing until instructed to do so by the shunter accompanying the move. The shunter must obtain an assurance from the   crossing keeper that the crossing is clear and the gates have been secured across the road before instructing the driver to proceed. *BR Eastern Region Sectional Appendix, 1969*

Above: With the church of St. John the Evangelist forming a backdrop, No. 51244 shunts Jubilee Quay by the large tranship shed which stood at this point. By 2001 there was no railway here and the area was devoted to containers. *Neville Stead.*

Besides the docks, run by the British Transport Docks Board, Goole had surprisingly few private sidings listed in the 1956 Stations Handbook. In fact, there were only two: Glossop & Bulay(1933) Ltd., connected to the NER line, and Lord Beverley's Siding at Oakhill, on the L&Y. In addition, there was Creyke's Siding, a public goods siding on the NE line between Goole and Thorne North.

Above: The almost 90 degree curves on some of Goole's dock lines demanded short wheelbase locomotives and the "Pugs" were ideal. When steam ended, they were replaced by three 200hp diesel hydraulic shunters built by the North British Locomotive Co. of Glasgow, represented here by D2701. The others were D2700 and D2702. Even these locos barely outlived steam, being withdrawn by 1967. *Peter Cookson.*

90

Above: West Dock on 12th October, 1988. The railway flanks both sides of this dock and in 2002 it is the only dock which is rail served, though track still crossed the road from the left side of West Dock into Railway Dock with its 50-ton rail-mounted crane. *Stephen Chapman*

In summer 1957, ferry services operated by Associated Humber Lines Ltd. (Goole Steam Shipping) left Goole for Amsterdam, Rotterdam and Antwerp on Wednesdays, and for Antwerp, Ghent, Hamburg and Copenhagen on Saturdays. Ferries arrived from Rotterdam and Hamburg on Mondays, and from Copenhagen on Saturdays, and from Antwerp on Wednesdays and Saturdays. There was no passenger service from Amsterdam to Goole. All these services were in fact provided by cargo ships and passenger accommodation was limited. By summer, 1961, sailings had been altered to three sailings from Goole to Bremen and three from Hamburg per fortnight, and one each way between Goole and Copenhagen on Fridays. They were still provided by cargo ships.

GOOLE SCISSORS CROSSING. The scissors crossing at the 40-ton coaling crane road and the curve immediately east of this crossing may be used by the following engines:
Standard Class 7 0-8-0 freight tender
Standard Class 4 2-6-0 freight tender
Standard Class 4 0-6-0 freight tender
Standard Class 3 0-6-0 freight tank
Standard Class 2 0-6-2 dock tank
and all former L&Y types.

LMS Central Division Sectional Appendix, 1937.

25 TON CRANE AND LOW END ROAD CROSSINGS.
Drivers requiring to work trips over these crossings must not foul the crossings, although the fixed signals may have been lowered, until hand-signalled forward by the ground staff. *LMS Central Division Sectional Appendix, 1937.* The same instruction still appeared in the BR Eastern Region 1969 Appendix by which time the crane was referred to as 50 ton.

SHORT MEMORIES

18.3.67: A Britannia Pacific passes through Selby with a Barrow-Hull football special. On the return it runs via Goole because a Dutch cargo ship is stuck in mud beneath Selby bridge preventing it being closed. ECML trains are diverted via Knottingley.

Above: The Lancashire & Yorkshire Railway formed a direct coast to coast railway from Goole Docks in the east to Liverpool Docks in the west and this was the eastern extremity, still with plenty of railway interest when photographed on 12th October, 1988. The single line heading towards the big shed marked Port of Goole leads to the north side of West Dock while the lines on the right lead to the south side and across the road to the coal shipping hoist and Railway Dock. Goole Goods Junction signal box on the right must have been the most easterly on the L&Y. The 350hp 0-6-0 shunter moving steel carrier wagons is 08177 while a Class 37 loco can be seen in the left distance on the loop just south of Boothferry Road.

By 2001, the signal box had gone along with all signalling, the sidings on the left were rationalised and the usual trees had overtaken the area to the point where it looked like a jungle, even though the railway was still active. Goole normally requires just one shunter nowadays, usually stabled by the former Bridge Street crossing when not in use. *Stephen Chapman*

Left: When coal was shipped from Goole, loaded wagons were shunted up to this hoist and the contents tipped into waiting ships. This was the Railway Dock shipping hoist on 12th October, 1988, very much disused. Out of the picture, to the left, the embankments and arches giving rail access from the lines in the West Dock area had been cleared. The hoist remains in 2001 as a monument to Goole's past. *Stephen Chapman*

Above: The view from behind the photographer taking the picture opposite. It shows the former L&Y yard on 12th October, 1988. The scene looks busy but the vans on the left had been in store for some time, taking advantage of considerable spare capacity which also saw withdrawn locomotives stored there at times. The wagons on the right are more genuine, some steel carriers are loaded while in the far distance is a rake of Cartic car carriers used to convey imported Renault cars, by the 13.57 Speedlink freight to York Dringhouses, from a terminal opened just a few years earlier at Potter's Grange. The far end of the yard connects to the Wakefield line, just beyond the bridge carrying the NER line over the top. The Knottingley & Goole Canal is on the left. By 2001, most of the yard was very overgrown though some wagons were still stored there and some of it was still in use. *Stephen Chapman*

Below: Goole yard from the south end looking towards the docks on 9th May, 1965 with Goole Mineral Junction signal box on the right. *Peter Rose*

Left: Among the dazzling array of shunters allocated to Goole over the years were the ex-Midland Railway 1F 0-6-0Ts of 1878 vintage for shunting and short trip working.
Here, No. 41855, the number barely readable through the grime, works pilot 23 turn, shunting Goole Yard at Mineral Junction. The North Eastern line to Thorne and Doncaster runs over the top. *Neville Stead*

DOWN FREIGHT TRAINS requiring to attach or detach traffic at Goole will receive instructions from the Canal Sidings foreman at Engine Shed Junction box. Trains departing from the marshalling sidings for Hull will be propelled from Mineral Junction to Engine Shed Junction thence via the Down line towards Boothferry Road. *BR Eastern Region (Northern Area)Sectional Appendix, 1969*
For the benefit of detaching wagons from Down trains on the NE line, up to 45 wagons could be propelled on the Up line from Potter's Grange to Engine Shed Jn. with or without a brake van.

Below: This was the view looking west from the NE line overbridge on 29th January, 1967. It shows the Engine Shed Junction area with the shed, still an active steam depot, and Engine Shed signal box at the centre of the scene. On the left are Canal Sidings and the Knottingley & Goole Canal while the double track diverging to the right leads up to Potter's Grange Junction.
The scene is very different in 2002. Just a single line comes in from the west and turns up to Potter's Grange while a disused and overgrown track continues under the NE line into Goole Yard from what remains of the junction. *Peter Rose*

Above: Another type of shunting loco to have graced Goole. More at home than the previous example, ex-L&Y 2F 0-6-0ST No. 51361 works alongside Engine Shed box on 21st April, 1956.

Below: This fabulous view, taken from the water softener at Goole engine shed on the same day, looks back towards Engine Shed Junction and the intersection with the NE line. The line of wagons curving left denotes the goods line up to Potter's Grange which was upgraded to passenger use in 1970. The fresh brickwork on the shed shows that it had recently been rebuilt.
Both P.B.Booth/N.E.Stead collection

Above: This British Railways photo taken from the coaling plant on 4th August, 1955 during roof reconstruction gives a good view of Goole engine shed and the surrounding district, known to railwaymen as "Sleepy Hollow." Goole's ubiquitous WD 2-8-0s predominate on shed, together with an Ivatt Class 2 2-6-0(left), a "Crab" 2-6-0(2nd left) and an L&Y 0-6-0ST(right.) Down below are narrow gauge tubs for removing loco ash. Beyond the turntable are Beverley Sidings where most incoming freights from the Wakefield direction arrived, while across the open ground on the right, beyond the water softener, is the line from Rawcliffe Bridge and Oakhill junctions to Boothferry Road which carried all the Goole-Wakefield, Leeds and Selby passenger trains. Rawcliffe Bridge Junction is in the far distance on the left while, for those with a keen eye, Oakhill Junction signal box is just visible about half way along the back of the trees behind the shed.

Goole shed's prime function was to provide goods engines for working over the L&Y line to the West Riding and shunting engines for the docks and local yards. It also had an allocation of smaller engines for local trip workings, including the Axholme Joint, and a small number of locos for passenger duties.

It was coded 25C in the Wakefield district of BR's London Midland Region until 1957 when it was transferred to the North Eastern Region's York district and coded 50D.

In 1954/55 the shed was reroofed and heightened to accommodate overhead electrical equipment such as cranes. The brick walls were strengthened with reinforced concrete pillars to support the pre-stressed concrete roof beams.

One of Yorkshire's last steam sheds, it closed to steam in summer, 1967 but continued to house diesels for a couple more years. It lost its own main line allocation with the end of steam and used Class 37 locos outbased from Hull Dairycoates, but retained its own shunters. The shed closed altogether at the end of 1969 after which shunters were stabled and refuelled at the former NE goods shed next to Goole station. In that guise, Goole retained its 50D shedcode and lasted long enough to receive the new TOPS code GO but locomotives were last allocated there in February, 1973.

The L&Y shed was demolished soon after total closure and by 1975 the site had become a railhead for stone brought from the Tilcon quarries near Skipton for construction of the M62 motorway. That traffic eventually ceased, the railhead was abandoned and the site became just one more tract of open scrubland.

LOCOMOTIVES ALLOCATED TO GOOLE, 25C, September, 1950

2P 4-4-0: 40586/9; **Fowler Class 4 2-6-4T:** 42411; **4F 0-6-0:** 44062/44105/44220/44485; **Ivatt 2MT 2-6-0:** 46405/07/8/9/37; **8F 2-8-0:** 48449/48738/68; **0F 0-4-0ST:** 51207/22/41/4; **2F 0-6-0ST:** 51323/61/ 79/51432/ 51516/ 51521; **Barton Wright 2F 0-6-0:** 52037/56; **Aspinall 2F 0-6-0:** 52133/52273/52592; **WD 2-8-0:** 90228/62/81. Total: 34

Above: A BR photo taken on 20th May, 1954 showing the engine shed before reconstruction, with its corrugated iron roof cladding. Just inside, behind ex-L&Y 2F 0-6-0ST No.51516 is Stanier Class 4 2-6-4T No. 42553, one of Goole's small stud of passenger engines, used mainly for Wakefield or Leeds trains.

Below: A line of Ivatt Class 4 2-6-0s and Hunslet Class 05 diesel shunters inside the shed on 9th May, 1965. The two steam locos are 43125 and 43098. *Peter Rose.*

LOCOMOTIVES ALLOCATED TO GOOLE, 50D, June, 1961

Ivatt Class 4 2-6-0: 43097/8/43125; **Ivatt Class 2 2-6-0:** 46407/8/9/15/78; **3F 0-6-0T:** 47438/62/47581/9/ 47634; **0F 0-4-0ST:** 51222/41/4; **WD 2-8-0:** 90044/94/90160/86/90213/28/60/2/5/90475/8/90531/90704; **Hunslet 0-6-0 diesel:** D2598/9/D2600/1/2/9/10/1/3/4; **North British 0-4-0 diesel:** D2700/1/2. Total: 42

The diversity of smaller engines to be found on Goole shed during the 1950s:

Top:Being L&Y territory, ex-L&Y engines were the norm, like Aspinall 2F 0-6-0s Nos. 52305, 52319, 52244, 52154 and 52252. They were the last of their class to work at Goole and are seen stored on 9th June, 1960 pending withdrawal. *Peter Cookson / N. Stead colln.*

Centre: Possibly the most unlikely engines to find a home at Goole were the former Manchester Sheffield & Lincolnshire J10 0-6-0s, displaced from the Manchester area and sent to work the Axholme Joint. No. 65196 was on shed on 11th May, 1958. Behind it is Midland 1F 0-6-0T 41661. *David Holmes*

Bottom: Even the Great Northern had a look in. J50 0-6-0T No. 68912 stands outside the shed at 3.16pm on 25th January, 1959. *David Holmes*

Top: Ex-LMS 3F 0-6-0Ts were another class of shunter to make their home at Goole, but they did not last long. Transferred in during September, 1959 to replace older types, they were soon displaced by diesels and after a period in store were withdrawn or transferred away in September, 1961. Nos. 47581, 47634, 47438, 47462 and 47589 were in store on 13th April, 1961 along with "Pug" 0-4-0ST No. 51222. *Peter Cookson / N.E.Stead collection*

Left: The North Eastern moves in. But T1 4-8-0 hump shunt tank No. 69918 from Hull was just visiting on 11th May, 1958. Alongside is another shunter of NER pedigree, J72 No. 69008, just eight years old, being built by BR in 1950. *David Holmes.*

LOCOMOTIVES ALLOCATED TO GOOLE, 50D, November, 1966

WD 2-8-0: 90030/81/91/4/9/90132/72/90406/27/51
Hunslet 0-6-0 diesel: D2598/9/D2600/1/2/9/10/1/3/4/6
North British 0-4-0 diesel: D2701/2
Ruston & Hornsby 0-4-0 diesel: D2957   Total: 24

Number taking: Down trains arriving 6am Monday to 6am Sunday must stop at Beverley Sidings, and at Mineral Junction from 6am Sunday to 6am Monday, for number taking purposes. Engines working wagons to the docks from Goole Junction, and all trains departing from Goole(except empty coal wagons, which will be recorded for the number taking at Beverley Sidings)must stop at Mineral Junction for number taking....*LMS Central Division Sectional Appendix, 1937.* Under this instruction in the BR North Eastern Region 1960 Appendix, Goole Junction was given as Potter's Grange.

The short-lived diesel era at Goole shed:
Left: Even after the end of steam, there was no let up in Goole's diversity of shunters.
In the shed with the Hunslets on 28th January, 1968 was Yorkshire Engine Co. Class 02 0-4-0 dock shunter No. D2865.
An influx of standard Class 03 and 04 0-6-0 diesel mechanical shunters, mostly in 1968 and 1969, finally put an end to this diversity.
Adrian Booth

LOCOMOTIVES ALLOCATED TO GOOLE, 50D, January, 1973

Class 03 0-6-0 diesel: 2151/2/7/69/73 Total: 5

All locos transferred to Hull Botanic Gardens by February, 1973.

Below: Standing outside the shed on 30th August, 1969, Hull Dairycoates Class 37s Nos. 6739 and 6784. Goole had no main line loco allocation from the end of steam but some Dairycoates 37s were outbased there.
Adrian Booth.

At the end of 1958, BR 350hp 0-6-0 diesel shunters Nos. 13233, D3675 and D3676 took over shunting duties at Goole previously carried out by the Midland 1F 0-6-0Ts. The three diesels were maintained at Hull Dairycoates shed until fuel storage tanks were installed at Goole. Each could spend a fortnight at Goole before having to return to Hull for fuel. They were soon replaced, however, by the smaller Hunslet locos.
Also in 1958, plans were laid to replace the three ex-L&Y "Pug" 0-4-0ST dock shunters with three North British 200hp 0-4-0 diesel hydraulic locos transferred from Hartlepool. No. 11702(later D2702), arrived at Goole for trials in early December.

Above: Rawcliffe Bridge, on the L&Y line to Wakefield, was the western extremity of the Goole railway system. This is the junction and signal box looking east. The goods lines to Beverley Sidings, Engine Shed Junction and the docks go straight ahead, while the passenger line goes left for 1152 yards to Oakhill Junction where it joins the NER line from Selby before continuing to Boothferry Road. Since the line via Oakhill Junction was abandoned, passenger trains from Leeds have run via Engine Shed Junction. *N.E.Stead collection.*

The line from Rawcliffe Bridge to Boothferry Road was 2 miles 901 yards long, signalling was Absolute Block and the maximum line speed 40mph.

The goods lines between Rawcliffe Bridge, Engine Shed Junction and Potters Grange were upgraded to passenger lines with Absolute Block signalling with effect from January, 1970, comensurate with closure of the existing passenger line from Rawcliffe Bridge to Boothferry Road via Oakhill Junction.

RAWCLIFFE BRIDGE-BEVERLEY SIDINGS

Not signalled by Absolute Block or Permissive Block on Down Hump Line - worked by telephone. Drivers must enter and run upon the undermentioned lines at a slow speed and be prepared to stop short of any obstruction.

Where there are no fixed signals at the exit end, drivers must not foul the connection until they are signalled forward by hand signal by the foreman or shunter. *LMS Central Division Sectional Appendix, 1937.*

In 1937, the Goole-Hensall Junction section of the L&Y line to Wakefield was signalled by Absolute Block except that there was No Block or Bell on the Down Goods line between Rawcliffe Bridge and Engine Shed Jn., and on the Up Goods between Beverley Sidings and Rawcliffe Bridge. Permissive Block was used for all non-passenger trains between Rawcliffe Bridge Jn. and Goole Goods Jn. Beverley Sidings-Rawcliffe Station was worked by Absolute Block when Rawcliffe Bridge signal box was closed.

There were signal boxes at Goole Goods Junction, Goole Mineral Jn., Engine Shed, Beverley Sidings, Rawcliffe Bridge Jn., Rawcliffe, Snaith East, Snaith West and Hensall Jn. Gate boxes which were not block posts were situated at Snaith Road level crossing and Snaith Church Lane crossing.

Additional running lines were Down Goods Rawcliffe Bridge-Mineral Jn., Down Goods Mineral Jn.-Goole Goods Jn., and Up Goods Beverley Sidings-Rawcliffe Bridge Jn. There were Lie-by(refuge) sidings at Snaith East(Down) for 36 wagons, engine and brake van, and at Snaith West(Up) for 26 wagons, engine and brake van.

By the end of the 1960s, Snaith East box had been abolished. Maximum line speed was 50mph.

Left: A feature of the A614 level crossing near Rawcliffe was the underpass which allowed cars to avoid being held up when the gates were across the road. Of course this option did not appeal much to railway enthusiasts. Here, Peter Rose preferred to wait at the gates and get a shot of 8F 2-8-0 No.48274 on 12th October, 1964.

Right: Rawcliffe station layout in LMS days. The goods yard closed in 1965 and the station has been unstaffed since 1968. In 2002 the line is single track and only the main platform is in use. *Not to scale*

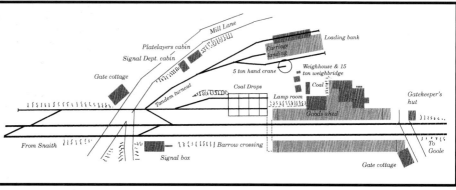

Below: Snaith station with a Leeds to Goole DMU calling in the late 1960s. Rationalisation has yet to take place though goods facilities, which included a 5-ton yard crane, were withdrawn in March, 1965. A private siding once served British Clog Sole Manufacturers Ltd. In the following years the track was singled, the station buildings demolished, Snaith West signal box(right) abolished and the level crossing converted to an open crossing with flashing warning lights. *Peter Cookson*

By the late 20th century, the passenger service was so sparse that the train was no longer a viable option for most people and the station had become a hang-out for local youths.

THE AXHOLME JOINT

Top: The classic view of Reedness Junction, 5 miles 1056yds from Goole, where the line to Haxey continued to the right and the branch to Fockerby went to the left. *G. Oates*

Right: Not much to see of Reedness Junction but the picture shows another example of Goole's diverse motive power. Ex-L&Y Barton Wright 0-6-0 No.52037 shunts the pick-up shortly after nationalization. *Norman Ling/P. Rose collection.*

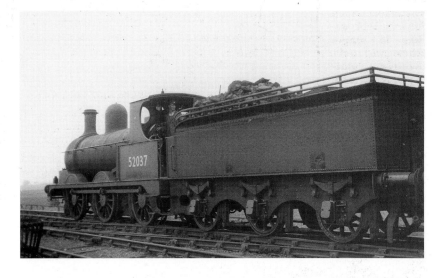

Left: Former Reedness Junction station master Norman Ling photographed this rare 1950s visitor to his station. Ex-NER N10 0-6-2T No. 69096 from Hull Dairycoates calls at the Haxey side with a Hull District inspection saloon.

SHORT MEMORIES

August 1967: 23 steam locos at Goole shed consist of B1s 61002,61255, 61289 and 20 WD 2-8-0s.

4.11.67: The 15.00 Carlton-Goole freight, hauled by Royston-based 8F 2-8-0 No. 48276, is the last working for an Eastern Region steam locomotive.

October 1968: The Goole-Wakefield line is still busy with freight. Traffic includes night trains between Hull and Healey Mills hauled by pairs of Class 20 diesels in the D83xx series.

Autumn 1974: Tate & Lyle unveil plans for a glucose factory at Howden Dyke with possible rail connection from Saltmarshe.

Above: The next station going south on the main line from Reedness Junction was Crowle, 8 miles 1100yds from Goole and some distance north of the bridge over the Doncaster-Grimsby line. The platforms are on the double track section and the goods yard on the extreme left in this view looking north. The 1956 Handbook of Stations showed Crowle as able to handle parcels and miscellaneous traffic, livestock, horse boxes and prize cattle vans, and carriages and motor cars by passenger and parcels train. *G. Oates.*

Below: This splendid view shows Ivatt Class 2 2-6-0 No. 46436 crossing Crowle swing bridge as it heads the pick-up towards Epworth. From left to right are Crowle Swing Bridge signal box, Keadby Canal and the Doncaster-Grimsby line. The bridge was powered by a 20hp Crossley oil engine but was demolished in 1972. Half a mile south of here was a 12-arch viaduct spanning the A18 Doncaster-Scunthorpe road, Double Rivers and the River Thorne, and beyond that a nine-arch viaduct over the New River Idle and drains. *G. Oates*

In the winter 1959/60 working timetable, the daily class K Axholme Joint pick-up goods was booked to leave Goole Sidings at 8.20am, call Goole Fields Siding when required and arrive Reedness Jn.at 9.1. It then served stations and sidings as required, first along the Fockerby branch and then via Epworth to Hatfield Moor. After returning from Hatfield Moor, the train was marshalled at Reedness Jn. into NE traffic first, then LMR traffic. It was booked to depart the junction at 2.30pm and arrive Goole Mineral Jn. 3.12.

Above: This view of Belton, 12 miles 1694yds from Goole, shows the simplicity of Axholme Joint stations - the low, basic platforms, timber building, station house and passing loop completing the scene plus, out of view, a capable goods yard which could handle a full range of traffic. Although closed to passengers, this station, like other Axholme Joint stations in the 1950s, was still open for parcels for which a barrow is kept on the platform. *G. Oates.*

Below: Judging by the smoke from the chimney, a welcoming coal fire is burning in the wooden station building at Epworth, but it won't be for the benefit of passengers as passenger services were withdrawn from the Axholme Joint in 1933. The goods yard on the right could handle furniture vans, portable engines, motor cars and machines on wheels in addition to those items that Crowle could deal with. Epworth was 14 miles 1694yds from Goole and as can be seen, since Reedness Junction the countryside has changed from totally flat to rolling hills. *G. Oates*

Above: The remote terminus at Hatfield Moor on 13th August, 1960 when Ivatt Class 2 2-6-0 No. 46407 arrived there with a party of enthusiasts travelling in two brake vans. *C. H. A. Townley*

Left: The other railway at Hatfield Moor. The extensive 3ft gauge system used to bring peat from the moor to the factory is still operating in 2002. Here, a Hunslet diesel, works No.7366, pushes wagons towards the tippler for unloading on 23rd April, 1977.
Stephen Chapman

The 1969 Appendix, showed the first call on a journey along the Axholme Joint to be Goole Fields siding followed by Reedness Jn. Next was Peat Works siding, then Spilman's siding(6 miles 1122yds from Goole) followed by Crowle, Hagg Lane coal siding, Belton and Epworth. Continuing to Hatfield Moor, Sandtoft depot was first, then Allerton's siding and finally the terminus at 19 miles 1386yds from Goole. From Reedness Jn. to Fockerby were Blackers siding, Whitgift's siding, Eastoft, Boltgate siding, Luddington, Pinder's siding, and Fockerby, 5 miles 1232yds from Reedness Junction.

The 1956 Stations Handbook lists six more sidings at Reedness: British Moss Litter, Corners, Dougherty's, Gossop's, Plum Tree Farm and Smith's. Between Crowle and Belton were Moor's Farm siding, Ealand public depot and Richard Thomas & Baldwin's. British Moss Litter had a siding at Hatfield Moor.

AXHOLME JOINT SIGNALLING, 1937

Reedness Jn.: Electric train staff(round, red) received from/handed to drivers by signalman at Marshland Jn. box and station master or competent clerk at Reedness.

Reedness Jn.-Haxey: Electric train tablet(round.) Token received/handed to drivers by station master/competent clerk at Crowle, Belton and Epworth token stations, and signalman at Haxey Jn.

Reedness Jn.-Fockerby: One Engine in Steam without key. On approaching Eastoft, drivers must whistle to warn staff.

Epworth-Hatfield Moor: Red square staff received from/handed to drivers by signalman at Epworth.

Maximum line speed 25mph(15mph if loco tender first), and 15mph on branches.

The Hatfield Moor and Fockerby branches were deleted from the Sectional Appendix by a supplement dated 4th May, 1970, and Marshland Jn.-Epworth by a supplement dated 8th February, 1975.

Above: The bare trees of winter strengthen the impression of a wild and windswept Isle of Axholme landscape as Ivatt Class 2 2-6-0 No. 46408 rests at Fockerby platform with the pick-up in the 1950s. Straw littering the foreground is evidence of the Axholme Joint's staple agricultural traffic.
G. Oates.

The impression of remoteness was increased by the entry in the 1956 Handbook of Stations which described the position of Fockerby station with the somewhat inprecise entry: "Branch near Goole." In spite of this, Fockerby was equipped to handle all types of freight traffic including parcels and, like all other Axholme Joint stations, must have been an important lifeline for farmers in this very fertile region. All rail traffic ceased with effect from 5th April, 1965 though the branch was retained along with the Marshland Jn.-Epworth section for some years afterwards.

Left: The end of the line. There could be no mistaking the road entrance to Fockerby goods depot as seen on 13th August, 1960, the day of the brakevan tour. The Bedford Doormobile van completes the contempory scene.
Hugh Davies

Above: Gascoigne Wood signal box has survived all the many changes which have taken place there since the 1960s while the curve to Milford is still occasionally used by diverted passenger trains, such as in December 2000/January 2001 when Hull-Manchester TransPennine services had to be rerouted via Castleford and Huddersfield to avoid major engineering work at Leeds City.

The occasion pictured here was on Sunday 19th August, 1980 when North East-South West expresses were diverted via Selby and Milford because of engineering work south of Church Fenton. At this time, Gascoigne Wood yard was used for wagon storage and engineers' traffic and BR/Sulzer Type 4 "Peak" Class 45 diesel No. 45007 was busy with a spoil train. The express, the 08.19 York-Bristol, was hauled by a Class 47 loco. *Stephen Chapman*

MODERN MEMORIES

Below: Milford on 20th January, 1980 when remodelling was under way in connection with the Selby Coalfield project and a Class 45 loco and steam crane were present. Soon the semaphore signals will have gone and there will be more sidings, replacing Gascoigne Wood yard which will become the loading railhead for the five mines making up the coalfield. *Robert Anderson*

Right: Church Fenton goods depot closed on 3rd October, 1966 but the buildings survived in private use, if trackless, in 1997. This view on 1st May shows the weighbridge house with the goods shed behind.

Below: Church Fenton station building in use as the Passage to India restaurant on 1st May, 1997. The entrance to the booking hall which closed when the station was de-staffed in November, 1988, is just under the BR logo.

Bottom: With its steep steps down to the platform, Ulleskelf station was not so passenger friendly. Still, it is being by-passed(as it is by most trains) by preserved A4 Pacific No. 4498 *Sir Nigel Gresley* as, whistle blowing, it tops 60mph along the Up Leeds line with an A4 Society special on 30th April, 1977.

The late 1990s saw the steps replaced with a huge steel ramp.

All by Stephen Chapman

Above: The view looking south at a much rationalised Selby South on 27th July, 1974. Deltic No. 55020 *Nimbus* passes a wilderness while on its way from King's Cross to Newcastle. Canal Yard, above the coaches, has all but disappeared while the site of the engine shed on the immediate right is similarly overgrown. By 2001 all but the main running lines was either abandoned or overgrown while the Leeds line curving off to the right now runs through what has become a dense forest. Just two disused sidings remain on the left. *J.C.Hillmer*

Below: A fine panoramic view of Selby station on 27th July, 1974, taken from the overbridge which passes over the south end. It shows the goods yard and original station still complete and handling a small amount of traffic, a local DMU for Leeds in the former Goole bay, and Class 31 diesel No. 31146 with a train bound for Sheffield. The 31 had failed and was about to be rescued by a pair of Class 25s. *J.C.Hillmer*

Above: Recalling the kind of status which Selby enjoyed until fairly recent times. A High Speed Train forming an InterCity 125 service to King's Cross accelerates along the Up Main away from the swing bridge on 9th May, 1981 as a Metro-Cammell Class 101 DMU prepares to leave with a local service to York. At least since 2000 an HST calls at Selby each way with GNER's Hull-King's Cross service. Non-stop trains can no longer pass through on the centre roads as they were lifted following the opening of the Selby Diversion in 1983. *Stephen Chapman*

Right: Pooley weighing machines were part and parcel of practically every station in the North Eastern Region. This survivor, seen in June, 1994, still forms part of a pleasing display on the Down platform at Selby, having helped local staff win best kept station awards in 1990 and 1994. *Stephen Chapman*

Below: In 1989, after it had been rammed by the 3000 ton Swedish cargo vessel Samo, BR undertook a £2 million refurbishment of Goole swing bridge. Here, during August, floating crane *London Atlas* lifts a new 30 tonne steel beam into position. *Stephen Chapman*

Opposite: A extract from the February, 1975 BR Eastern Region Sectional Appendix supplement setting out instructions for operating the new Tilcon stone terminal at Goole.

Centre: Thorne North station in September, 1999, still retaining its buildings, small canopy and NER style footbridge, but no staff. The Class 142 is leaving for Doncaster.

Bottom: In the early 1920s the NER tried using a Leyland bus body on rail wheels on the Cawood service. After 80 years of progress, the 13.50 Goole to Leeds enters Snaith formed of a Leyland bus body on rail wheels. Since this scene on 17th April, 1993, the Class 141 railbuses introduced in the 1980s have been withdrawn, some being exported to Iran but their descendants, the Class 142s, roll on.

This is all that remains of the once busy L&Y line to Goole and even since this picture was taken, the remnants of the goods yard have been sept away. In late 2001, this line became disused when its two daily trains each way were replaced by buses due to a shortage of train drivers. What more can one say.
Both Stephen Chapman

GOOLE ENGINE SHED JN. TILCON DEPOT. The connection to Tilcon Ltd. depot is situated in the Down Main at Engine Shed Junction, between Nos. 37(First Home) and 36(Second Home) signals and is ground frame controlled, electrically released from Engine Shed Junction signal box.....

The depot consists of one long siding....An elevated hopper for wagon discharge is situated along the siding.....Trains to the depot will comprise of up to 30 wagons.

A train for the depot will be brought to a stand at No.37 signal, the guard must alight and the train must draw forward clear of the siding connection. The train must be propelled into the depot under the authority of signal No.22 and must be brought to a stand in the depot clear of the ground frame connection to enable the guard to normalise the ground frame before the train is propelled forward up to the marker board midway to the hopper.... a batch of three wagons at one time will be discharged.

After leaving the depot, the train will proceed to Goole Yard for the locomotive to run round and for C &W examination.